BASIC PRINCIPLES OF ECONOMIC VALUE

BASIC PRINCIPLES OF ECONOMIC VALUE

EUGEN VON BÖHM-BAWERK

Translated by
Hans F. Sennholz

from
Grundzüge der Theorie des wirtschaftlichen Güterwerts
in Conrad's
Jahrbücher für Nationalökonomie und Statistik,
New Series, Volume 13, 1886.

Libertarian Press, Inc.
P.O. Box 309
Grove City, PA 16127
(724) 458-5861

ISBN 0-910884-46-3

MANUFACTURED IN THE UNITED STATES OF AMERICA

CONTENTS

PREFACE

During his lifetime Eugen von Böhm-Bawerk (1851-1914) enjoyed an illustrious reputation as both statesman and economist. As an official of the Austrian Ministry of Finance he was instrumental in reforming the income tax; as the Vice-President of a special commission he guided the country in its return to the gold standard, and as Minister of Finance he insisted on the elimination of all sugar subsidies. He rose to this illustrious rank no fewer than three times. He resigned from his third appointment, precipitating the fall of the administration, when increased financial demands of the Austrian army endangered the balancing of the budget. When he was offered the most lucrative position in government, the post of Governor of the Central Bank, he rejected the offer in favor of a professorship at the University of Vienna.

The publication of his three-volume *Capital and Interest* established Böhm-Bawerk's reputation as one of the great economists of the 19th century. His contemporaries used to compare his importance with that of David Ricardo whose rigidly deductive method of analysis served as a model for subsequent work by Austrian economists. Böhm-Bawerk paved the way for a better understanding of the process of production and especially the nature of capital and interest. He was trusted and admired during his lifetime, but forgotten or ignored when World War I ravaged the great Western powers and soon thereafter the doctrines of Karl Marx and John Maynard Keynes began to sway the minds of the people. But his theories live on not only in the writings of Austrian economists but also wherever economic principles are being discussed and formulated.

Economic value was the *causa prima* for Böhm-Bawerk; all other economic phenomena merely rest and build on economic value. Carl Menger had affirmed marginal utility as the foundation of economic valuation and action and developed an atemporal theory of value, allocation, and exchange. In his footsteps, Böhm-Bawerk constructed a system that combined the Menger concepts with his analysis of roundabout method of production. He took issue with his senior for explaining interest income as earnings flowing from the "power of disposal over quantities of economic goods within a definite period of time." To Böhm-Bawerk, a "power-of-disposal theory" was rather inadequate and unable to lead to a satisfactory explanation of interest.

The first volume of the trilogy was *History and Critique of Interest Theories* (1884) which brilliantly analyzed various interest theories from ancient times to his days. He disproved the "productivity theories" of J.B. Say and his many followers in France, Germany, and Italy. He countered the "motivated" productivity theories of Lord Lauderdale and Thomas R. Malthus. He rebutted especially what he called the "abstinence theories" of the Classical economists Adam Smith, David Ricardo, Nassau Senior, and Frederic Bastiat. He meticulously exploded the "exploitation theories" of Pierre Proudhon, John Stuart Mill, Karl Marx, and their many disciples. Realizing that he had to build a solid theoretical foundation for his cold critiques, he penned the indispensable and fundamental basis of his theme, this very essay, *Basic Principles of Economic Value*; it was published in the most important economic journal of its time, in Conrad's *Jahrbücher* in 1886. It was reprinted forty-six years later, in German, in the School of Economics, *Series of Scarce Tracts in Economic and Political Science*, Number 11, London, 1932.

Böhm-Bawerk further elaborated his analysis in the second volume called *Positive Theory of Capital* (1889). When members of the German Historical School summarily rejected his inquiry, he continued to pen several essays in support of his value theory or as critical commentary on the writings of other economists. They first appeared in later editions of *Positive Theory of Capital* in 1909 and 1912 and in a separate volume called *Further Essays on Capital and Interest* in a posthumous edition in 1921.

The writings of Böhm-Bawerk provided significant support to his senior colleague Karl Menger who was embroiled in a bitter dispute with the German Historical School. Professors Gustav

Schmoller, Albert Schäffle, and many others rejected the abstract-deductive method of Classical economics and instead sought empirical historical knowledge about different societies and countries under different circumstances and at different times. They formed a broad movement eager to shape public opinion and participate in political activity for social reform. Known as the "socialists of the chair," they paved the way for the German welfare state that set the example for all others around the globe.

In his *Principles of Economics*, Professor Menger had sought to demonstrate that the central point of economics is the phenomenon of value and that economic theory seeks to discover and explain the causal relationships between economic goods and human values. He had hoped to reach especially the German-speaking economic profession but was rebuffed summarily. To them, Menger's theory was not only incorrect but useless. Rejected and attacked, Menger replied with *Investigations into the Method of the Social Sciences with Special Reference to Economics* (1883) and, a year later, with an impassioned pamphlet entitled *The Errors of Historicism* (1884).

Böhm-Bawerk quietly reinforced Menger with this very essay, *Basic Principles of Economic Value*. Rewritten and enlarged, it was to constitute Book III of his *Positive Theory of Capital* (1889). It presents his basic thesis that all economic knowledge must build on a thorough inquiry into the nature of subjective value. In his own words, "our science, instead of ignoring subjective sensations, wants, etc. and subjective value based thereon, must search among them for the beginning of an explanation of all economic phenomena. A theory that fails to develop the theory of subjective value is built on quicksand." He laid the foundation and then elaborated the important role played by the passage of time in production. His time-preference theory was used, expanded, and perfected by other economists such as Knut Wicksell, Frank A. Fetter, and Irving Fisher. But it was left to Ludwig von Mises to extend and apply the subjective value theory also to money and indirect exchange, thereby completing the value theory. In their footsteps, reading and studying this essay is like conversation with one of the great economists of the last century.

During the 1950s and early 1960s Frederick Nymeyer, the personal friend of Ludwig von Mises and founder of Libertarian

Press, published most of Böhm-Bawerk's writings in English. His favorite translator was this writer who was attending Professor von Mises' classes at New York University. He translated this essay in 1960, but it did not reach the printers because in sum and substance it had already appeared in the Positive Theory of Capital in 1959. The Ludwig von Mises Institute under the direction of Llewellyn Rockwell now is the driving force for a completion of a Böhm-Bawerk collection in English.

February 2005 Hans F. Sennholz

INTRODUCTION

People who wish to study economic value face a problem from the outset, i.e., the ambiguity of the word "value."

Unfortunately, ambiguous terminology is commonplace in our science. Therefore, experienced theorists generally have the skill and aptitude to find their way through terminological ambiguity; however, this is not the case for the majority of scholars discussing economic value.

It seems to us that nearly all theorists are espousing one of two extremes, both of which do no justice to the case. Some, indeed, by far most of them, act as if there is no doubt or controversy on the value concept. Each one develops his own popular term, and neglects all others. There may be some variety in the form of neglect, but the result is always the same. Existence of value concepts other than a favored one may be completely ignored. Or, the existence of other concepts may be briefly mentioned, but only to censure them as fallacious, useless, or unscientific. And finally, one or another term is introduced formally, is classified or defined, but then left unused in the scientific system. It is well known that this is what happened to the term "use value" as well as its more fortunate competitor, "exchange value," in the writings of the English School from Adam Smith down to our day. Whether these terms adequately describe and contrast two basically different concepts remains unanswered for the moment.

Other writers have gone to the other extreme. They felt duty-bound to pursue with equal care all linguistic nuances of the value concept. The most distinguished representative of this less numerous group is J. Neumann.[1] In Schoenberg's *Handbook of Political Economy*. He listed no fewer than a dozen meanings of the value term and then endeavored to incorporate them in the vocabulary of economics.

It seems to me that neither one of these extremes is very satisfactory. Those people who prefer a single concept while neglecting all others merely do justice to one aspect of the scientific problems. Their value theories are bound to remain incomplete. In addition, they may suffer the unfortunate fate, which has befallen most value theorists, that they cast their preferences for the more conspicuous but superficial term, while ignoring the fundamental and therefore scientifically more fruitful concept. They may thus investigate the surface of things and leave their roots in the dark, which renders their value theories not only incomplete but also rather unsatisfactory. This appraisal mainly concerns the theories of the English School and its numerous followers who brush aside as scientifically unsuited the "subjective use value" and pursue exclusively the "objective exchange value."

The position of some other theorists is more propitious. Messrs. Menger[2] and more recently also Wieser[3] present a comprehensive theory of subjective value while sidelining the objective value concepts. They have the advantage of attacking the problem at its proper end, the root. They first develop the fundamental concepts and principles and thereby gain the key to more complicated phenomena. But the unfortunate perplexity of terminology causes these more comprehensive theories to appear incomplete, at least upon superficial examination. This weakens their credibility and persuasiveness.

Of course, all the findings of those theories pertain only to *subjective value*, because that is all they are investigating. However, the term "value" in popular usage frequently has objective connotations, and people expect value theories to explain

---

[1] 2nd edition, p. 156 *et seq.*

[2] *Grundsätze der Volkswirtschaftslehre* (*Principles of Economics*), Vienna 1871, Chapter III.

[3] *Ursprung und Hauptgesetze des wirtschaftlichen Wertes* (*Origin and Main Principles of Economic Value*), Vienna 1884.

objective value. The subjective value theories offer no such explanation, which may cause them to appear incomplete. Or they may seem fallacious if, without further examination, the findings on subjective value are applied to objective value and then, of course, found to be inapplicable. I am convinced that it is mainly these misconceptions that are responsible for such a slow professional acceptance of the profound and fruitful concept of economic value as developed by such scholars as Menger, Jevons, and Wieser.[4]

Other scholars suffer from a different misfortune. By closely imitating the popular usage, they introduce into economics as many independent value concepts as there are language nuances. These authors who seem to mistake the task of a linguist for that of an economist smother theory with superabundance. By elaborating all too many concepts they are prevented from analyzing thoroughly any one of them.

The example of J. Neumann offers cogent proof. This distinguished scholar of economic principles fills no fewer than 17 large pages of Schoenberg's *Handbook* with his sagacious and often pertinent analyses. But if you were to look for a genuine theory of value, for thorough investigations of the source of value, or for the conditions and laws of its magnitude, you will be greatly surprised that this most important material has found no place in the most comprehensive and profound systematic magnum opus of German economic literature.[5]

The following discussion suggests the proper medium between the two extremes. Economic science faces the task of explaining economic phenomena. To this end it must adapt all its scientific methods and therefore also its concepts. Furthermore, it must develop and cherish any concept needed for its explanation and exclude terms that lack scientific application. To be more specific, economic science must accept all those, and only those value concepts that have economic significance. This includes concepts

---

[4] 2nd edition, p. 156 - 173.

[5] Or should this strange omission not be traced back to the author of the specific sections on the "value concept" and the "formation of prices," but to an oversight when the whole treatise was outlined?

that either are derived directly from economic phenomena or are important for an explanation of other economic phenomena.

When viewed from this perspective, economic science must utilize *two* concepts both of which portend value in popular usage although they differ fundamentally from each other. Let us distinguish them as *subjective* and *objective* value.[6]

Value in the subjective sense is the significance which an economic good or a number of goods possesses for the well-being of an individual. In this sense a good is valuable to me when I perceive it to be significant for my well-being. This means that its possession satisfies a want, affords a pleasure or comfort, or saves me from a pain which I would have to suffer without the good. In this case, possession of the good constitutes a gain and its loss signifies a reduction of my well-being. It is important to me, it has value for me.

Value in the objective sense means the power or ability of a good to achieve an objective result. In this sense there are as many kinds of value as there are results. There is a nutrition value of foods, a heat value of wood and coal, a fertilizer value of various manures, a blast value of various explosives, etc. All these value terms lack any reference to the well-being of an individual. When we say that beech wood has a higher heat value than pine, we state a purely objective or "mechanical" fact. We are simply stating that a certain quantity of beech wood yields more heat than the same quantity of pine wood. Therefore, instead of the value term we also use the synonyms "power" or "capacity," which point up the purely objective relationship. Instead of "nutrition value" we may say "nutritional potency," "heat capacity" instead of "heat value," "blasting force" instead of "explosive value," etc.[7]

These examples of objective value do not refer to economic relationships but to purely physical conditions. And although they frequently appear in economics textbooks they do not concern

---

[6] I am here following the very suitable terminology of Neumann (*ibid.*, p. 157) from which, however, I deviate considerably in the various branches of the main division mentioned above.

[7] This is well presented by Mr. Wolf in an essay "On the Theory of Value," which probably will appear simultaneously with this publication and which the author has kindly made available to me.

economic science. It is not the task of economics to explain the heat capacity of wood, or to use any other physical or technical fact in its explanation of economic phenomena. I mentioned these examples only to illustrate more clearly that objective value plays an eminent role in economics: the *objective exchange value of goods.*

This is the objective significance of goods in exchange, or in other words, their capacity to obtain in exchange a quantity of other economic goods, which is a power or property.[8] In this sense we may say, this house is worth $100,000 or that horse $500 because in exchange we may obtain $100,000 or $500 respectively. Again, as in the case of heat value, we do not refer to the effect the goods may have on the well-being of an individual. We merely denote the objective fact that a certain good obtains a certain quantity of other goods in exchange. And we may observe again that the word "value" can be replaced by the synonym "power." The English speak of "purchasing power," The Germans are beginning to use the word "Tauschkraft."

Exchange value is not the only member of the objective value group that refers to economic effects, although it is by far the most important one. We may ascribe economic significance also to terms such as "yield value," "production value," "rent value," etc. But they have no special scientific benefit. Our science, therefore, does well enough by merely mentioning them. It need not develop a comprehensive theory of yield or production value. In my judgment, this task must be reserved to the abovementioned value concepts: the subjective value and the objective exchange value. I need not prove that the latter demands a thorough investigation. For there is unanimous agreement that it is one of the most important tasks of economic theory to clarify the exchange relations of goods or, what is called, the object exchange value, and to develop its laws. But there is less agreement on the need today to develop a comprehensive theory for subjective value. To set forth not only this theory but also its indispensability and scientific benefit is one of the most important tasks of the following pages.

We have been speaking of subjective and objective value as if

[8] Cf. Wolf, ibid.

they were two entirely independent concepts instead of two links of a single general value concept. Is this really the case? Is it not possible to develop a fundamental concept that encompasses both and thus saves our science the embarrassment of bestowing the same ambiguous name on two completely different concepts?

Like Neumann,[9] I deem this utterly impossible. "Importance for the well-being of an individual" and "objective power of exchange for other goods" are two concepts that have in common so few logical characteristics that a common comprehensive concept would have to be quite vague and useless. This is not to deny that both have some internal and external relationships. And both undoubtedly have sprung from the same root. But this union must be traced back in the history of language. In the present it is lost through a differentiation of terms that took place more recently. It is indeed very likely that one of the terms gradually developed from the other one. Perhaps the subjective meaning "importance for an individual" was originally the only one. Later, while elaborating the kinds and nature of economic utility, one began to include the objective results on which the subjective importance depends (value = importance depending on exchange power, heat power, nutrition potency, etc.). And finally, one tended to eliminate the subjective factor through an ambiguous manner of speech and grew accustomed to connect the value term with certain objective capabilities of things (value = exchange power, heat power, nutrition potency, etc.) Perhaps the value term originally referred exclusively to exchange and then was transmitted to other conditions. Only those goods may have been deemed valuable that yielded a high return in exchange, or perhaps only those goods that otherwise are significant for human well-being were deemed valuable.[10]

The question of which one of these development processes actually took place may be left to the linguist. For the economist as such it has little interest. He merely needs to bear in mind that no matter what the common root of the value concept may have been,

---

[9] *Ibid.*, p. 156.

[10] Wolf is quoting Wigand (ibid.) who writes that the old-Nordic "vërd" originally meant "release price," then "price." This would indicate that the second variant is the most probable one.

today's concepts differ so widely that it is no longer feasible to unite them in one comprehensive scientifically beneficial term.

Like the explanation of terms so must the theories of value differentiate themselves. The two independent groups of phenomena require two equally independent theories. It is rather unfortunate that both must deal with their different subject matters under the identical name of value. The confusion over value has caused countless errors and will undoubtedly cause more in the future. Unfortunately we cannot expect much improvement in the near future.

To deprive the subjective value of this name is completely out of the question.[11] In the first place, concept and term are closely entwined in scientific as well as popular language. Furthermore, we would not find a suitable replacement for this important concept. It would be easier to replace the objective value term with the short and significant term of "exchange power." I would even deem this most desirable although I would not want it adopted immediately because in popular usage the term value is as closely connected with its objective meaning as with the subjective one. To change this is not impossible, but certainly not easy - especially in the Romance languages in which valore, valeur, and value strongly remind us of the importance in exchange, more so than the German "Wert." And furthermore, it will be many years before a large majority of theorists not only grants equal rights to objective exchange power but also believe it to be the only legitimate bearer of the name value, the only "true economic value." Under these conditions an early rejection of the name value would merely tend to aggravate the misunderstandings which it is supposed to alleviate. Therefore, my proposals so far are limited to the term "exchange power" being accepted as the synonym for objective exchange value.[12]

---

[11] As, for instance, Jevons proposed in his *Theory of Political Economy*, 2nd edition, p. 82 *et seq*.

[12] If Wolf, *ibid*., admits the objective exchange value and even objective values only as "spurious," he expresses what I believe to be correct perception but dubious form. The truth is that those concepts belong to a category other than our "subjective" value, which Wolf names differently but perceives similarly. But to

(continued...)

The theory of value stands so to speak in the center of all economics. Nearly all important and perplexing problems, especially the great questions of income distribution, rent, wages, and interest, find their roots in the value theory. A final and undisputed solution of the value problem, therefore, would immediately advance our science in nearly all aspects. The number of attempts at its elucidation reflects the widely understood importance of the subject matter.

Unfortunately the success at solving the value problem has, until recently trailed by far that of the efforts. In spite of countless attempts the theory of value remained one of the most obscure, confused, and controversial parts of our science.[13] And it remains so today. But if I am not mistaken, a final change for the better is near. It seems to me that some recent literary efforts brought forth in the rising ferment the redeeming concept. Its development can be expected to offer the final solution. Under such circumstances I deem it timely to direct the attention of all scientists to this basic problem of economics. Furthermore, by building on foundations laid by distinguished predecessors I do hereby attempt to develop the main principles of a value theory in part by distinguishing between the theory of subjective value on the one hand and the objective exchange value on the other.

---

[12] (...continued)
declare the latter as the only legitimate bearer of the value name and to reject the former as "spurious" is a move that is out of step with the times.

[13] There is no more dramatic illustration of this sentence than the simple enumeration of various famous definitions of value. According to Rau, "value is the degree of ability of a good to serve human objectives." According to Roscher, "economic value of a good is its significance for the end in view of economizing man." According to Carey, "value is the degree of power of nature over man." According to Bastiat, "value is the relationship between two services exchanged." And according to Marx, "value is congealed labor time."

PART I

THE THEORY OF SUBJECTIVE VALUE

I

NATURE AND ORIGIN OF SUBJECTIVE VALUE

All goods have a certain bearing on human well-being. We distinguish between two different levels of this bearing. We speak of a lower level where a good merely has the *capability* of serving human needs. The higher level requires that a good be not only capable of causing a welfare effect but that it also be its indispensable *condition*, that is, the good's possession or loss provides or denies some material enjoyment. Our rich and sensitive language has coined different terms for both levels. The lower level is called *utility*, the higher level *value*.

There is a real difference. Let us make it as clear as possible because the distinction is of fundamental importance for the whole value theory.

One man is sitting near a spring that gushes good drinking water. His cup is filled and enough water runs by to fill a hundred cups. Another man is traveling in a desert. A long day's journey through hot desert sand still separates him from the nearest oasis. He has only a single cup of water, his last one. What is the difference between the two cups of water and the well-being to their owners?

It can be readily seen that the owners' relationship to their cups of water is very different. But what is the difference? In the former instance there is only the lower level of well-being, the utility; in the latter scenario there is also the higher level. The cup of water is useful, that is, capable of satisfying a need in both cases. And it does so equally. It is obvious that the water's refreshing attributes, i.e. its ability to quench a thirst, its coolness, taste, etc. are not at all weakened by the fact that other cups have identical attributes, nor are they enhanced by the fact that no additional water is available. But both cases differ materially relative to the second qualifying level of welfare condition. In the former case we must admit that the possession of the cup of water does not satisfy any additional wants, nor does its loss deprive our man of a single satisfaction. With the cup of water he can quench his thirst; without it he can quench it equally well with any one of the hundred other cups which the gushing spring freely provides every minute. He may make the first cup that is quenching his thirst the *cause* of his satisfaction. But under no circumstance is it an indispensable *condition*; it is dispensable, insignificant, and irrelevant for his well-being.

The second scenario is quite different. We must see that our desert traveler, without this last cup of water, would suffer from his exposure to the elements and perhaps succumb to them. His last cup of water is not only capable of causing a welfare effect but is also an indispensable condition, the *sine qua non* of well-being; it is considerable, important, and possesses great significance for his well-being.

I am not understating my case if I declare this difference to be one of the most fruitful and basic distinctions found in our science. It does not owe its existence to the magnifying glass of hair-splitting logicians. Rather, it is practiced by the people who instinctively know and use it, and allow it to direct their behavior toward economic goods, both in their intellectual understanding and their economic actions. Acting man behaves with indifference and carelessness towards goods that are merely useful. The academic knowledge that a good may be useful does not arouse a real interest in it when one also realizes that the same purpose can be accomplished without it. Such goods are insignificant for our well-being, and we treat them as such. We pay no attention to their loss and do not strive for their possession. Who would grieve about or try to prevent a cup of water from being spilled at the spring? But wherever we perceive that some satisfaction, well-being, or enjoyment depends on a good, our personal interest in it is piqued and we immediately take an interest in the good, which we believe will satisfy our desires. We project our own well-being into it, we recognize its significance as value to us, and finally, we make the necessary effort to acquire and keep it to further our well-being.

It is obvious that a science that is to explain man's actions toward material goods should elaborate, through development of a fundamental concept, the circumstances under which man cares for such goods. To be sure, man is selfish towards goods. He esteems, desires, or strives for goods not for their own sake, but because he seeks his own gratification. Therefore, the key to man's economic action is found in the bearing a desired good has on one's well-being. Just because a good is useful does not guarantee that it will improve well-being. This is why our science holds the clear and self-evident duty to separate the reason for action from mere utility and raise it to the status of a fundamental concept. Whether this is done using one term or another may be unimportant at this time. But it must be done for the sake of our scientific task, even if custom and language had not already laid the groundwork. If the concept "economic well-being that induces human action" were totally unknown, our science would have to create a word for it and introduce it. But this was not the case. We find the concept and the name already in use in popular language: they are embodied in the term *value*.

Our science has only recently recognized its good fortune which language provided by making the distinction between value and utility. While economics focused its full attention on the objective exchange value, it ignored subjective value and failed to distinguish it from the utility concept. At first, value and utility were used synonymously.[1] Later, a distinction was made, but only in language and not in fact. According to some writers, economic value was the utility recognized by man.[2] According to others, economic value was the degree of utility.[3] Eventually, some writers began to define economic value as the *significance* goods have to man.

This was an important step forward, however it was merely the

---

[1] Smith, Vol. I, Chapter IV; Ricardo, *Principles*, Vol. I, Chapter 1; Malthus, *Definitions*, Chapter II, def. 4, "Value in use is synonymous with utility." Also Hermann, *Staatswirtschaftliche Untersuchungen*, 1832, p. l.

[2] Storch, *Cours d'économie politique*, Paris 1823, Chapter I, p. 48; Friedlander, *Theorie des Wertes*, 1852, p. 48.

[3] Among others Rau, *Volkswirtschaftslehre*, 8th ed., I, p. 87; Knies, "Lehre vom Werth," *Zeitschrift für die ges. Staatswissenschaft*, 1855, p. 423.

first step and not the goal. In fact, Professor Schäffle, who deserves credit for a more comprehensive definition, did not fully understand this relationship. He did not base the significance of goods solely on their particular bearing on human well-being. Sometimes he attributed their significance to mere "usefulness"[4] and at other times on a mixture of utility and costs.[5] His successors also failed to take the next step. They continued to explain economic value as the importance ascribed to goods because of their ability to satisfy human wants.[6]

Once again, value was tied to the ability or capacity to satisfy human wants. The term "significance" seemed to sever value from individual well-being. And again, they made the mistake of ascribing importance to objects that in and of themselves can never contain importance. As we have seen above, a thing can be useful but it may nevertheless be completely irrelevant for our well-being. "Irrelevance" and "significance" are concepts that are mutually exclusive. It was left to Professor Menger to separate clearly and conclusively these confusing concepts. He thereby made one of the most significant and underappreciated contributions to economic theory.[7]

---

[4] *Tübinger Universitätsschriften*, 1862, Ch. 5, p. 10: "Value is the significance which a good has for the economic objective of economic man due to its utility."

[5] Ges. System, 3rd ed., Chapter I, p. 166 *et seq*.

[6] Cf. von Mangoldt's *Grundriss der Volkswirtschaftslehre*, 2nd ed. prepared by Kleinwächter. Von Mangoldt's discussion in his *Volkswirtschaftslehre*, 1868, (written for *Bibliothek der gesamten Handelswissenschaft*) is much better, yea even excellent: "Value is the significance attached to certain things that occur as a result of the evil that is suffered without them," p. 132.

[7] *Grundsätze der Volkswirtschaftslehre*, Vienna, 1871, p. 78: "Thus value is the significance which concrete goods or goods quantities acquire for us because we are or believe to be dependent on their possession for satisfaction of our wants." According to Menger, Professor Pierson, among others, joined our group with an excellent work on *Staathuishoudkunde*, Leerboek 1884,, I, p. 49 et seq; *Groundbeginselen*, 2nd ed., 1886, p. 312. Wieser built on the same foundation with his profound monograph on *Ursprung und Hauptgesetze des wirtschaftlichen Wertes*, Vienna, 1884. And partially also Wolf, *ibid*.

Not far behind Menger in clarity and completeness are the analyses of the sagacious leaders of the "mathematical school" of economics. Cf. especially

(continued...)

We have described the factors that create economic value and, therefore, can proceed to the formal definition. *Value is the importance a good possesses for individual well-being.* We need not expound on the nature and cause of this importance as goods can only acquire it in one way: by becoming the indispensable condition, the *conditio sine qua non* of any particular well-being. In other definitions value is frequently explained as "significance," which erroneously refers to the mere capacity to be useful or equally erroneously, to the "necessity of expenditure." Let *us* explain economic value with indubitable certainty as *the importance that a good or number of goods acquire for the well-being of an individual,*[8] *without which some satisfaction would have to be foregone.*

As frequently mentioned before, economic value is neither an objective quality inherent in goods, nor is it a purely subjective phenomenon that resides in the inner self of man.[9] Instead, it is a particular relationship between an individual and an object. If I call this concept "subjective value," I do not mean to deny the existence of objective factors. In fact, I would like to emphasize the strong and direct involvement of the subjective factor and thereby point out a substantial difference between our "subjective value" and the purely objective capacity of exchange and similar value concepts.

The lower level of a good's bearing on human well-being, that

---

[7] (...continued)
Jevons, *Theory of Political Economy*, 2nd ed., 1879, Ch. III, and all the writings by L. Walras. However, the old confusion has remained with many other recent authors. Even a theorist of Neumann's qualification defines value either as mere "capability" (Schönberg's *Handbook*, 2nd ed. p. 156, para. 6A) or "suitability" (ibid., p. 164., notes 4 and 5), or "significance" (pp. 163, 164). He thereby reveals that he is unaware of the essential difference between mere utility and value.

Among all these works those of Menger and Wieser are most relevant for modern value theory. I am using this opportunity to generally refer to them as excellent source material and to give express credit to them for some of the knowledge in this work.

[8] I need not emphasize that I am using the word "well-being" in its broadest sense, comprising not only the selfish interests of an individual but also everything desirable to him.

[9] Wolf, *ibid.*, raises proper objections, but with superfluous emphasis under the circumstances.

is, mere utility, is common to all goods. But the higher level, economic value, is specific to a particular good under certain circumstances. For value to emerge, utility must be accompanied by scarcity, which need not be absolute but must be relative to the demand for a particular good. To be more precise, *goods acquire value when the total supply of a particular good is so small that it is insufficient to meet the demand, or when the supply is at least so minimal that it is unable to satisfy the demand without the goods in question.*

In contrast, goods that are offered in such abundance as to cover not only all the wants they are capable of satisfying, but also provide an excess supply for which there is no demand, remain valueless. This excess supply must be large enough that the goods or quantities of goods in question can be spared without loss of any want satisfaction.

Proof for these tenets is not difficult after our introductory remarks on the nature of value. If insufficient quantities of goods are available so that some wants remain unsatisfied, it is obvious that the loss of a single good results in the loss of a gratification that otherwise would be possible. Conversely, the addition of a single unit affords a satisfaction that otherwise would be foregone. A certain satisfaction or well-being depends on the good.

The situation is obviously different when a surplus of goods exists. We would feel neither the loss of a single unit, which would immediately be covered by the surplus, nor the addition of one unit for which there is no useful employment. Let us assume, for instance, that a farmer requires a daily supply of 1000 gallons of water for all his needs, as well as the needs of his family and his help, his livestock, etc. But the single spring at his disposal produces only 800 gallons per day. It is obvious that he cannot forego a single gallon without suffering a loss in his economic objectives. Every gallon is a condition of well-being. This situation exists even with a daily supply of precisely 1000 gallons. But if the spring produces 2000 gallons daily, it is clear that the loss of a single gallon does not hurt our farmer in the least because he can profitably employ only 1000 gallons, he lets 1000 gallons run away unused. If 100 gallons are lost, they are replaced from the abundance. The only effect of losing 100 gallons is the reduction of the unused surplus from 1000 to 900 gallons.

Man concerns himself with the acquisition and possession of scarce goods. On the other hand, goods in abundant supply are freely available to everyone. Thus we may express the foregoing tenets in these words: *all economic goods have value, all free goods are worthless.* Let us keep in mind that *quantitative relations alone* determine whether a good merely is capable of rendering utility or also is a condition of well-being.

All free goods, we said, are worthless. Air and drinking water are such free goods. And yet, it is obvious that we cannot exist five minutes without air or one week without potable water. In fact, our well-being greatly depends on these free goods. How can that be?

This seems to be a contradiction. To explain it we must direct our attention to a fact that will confront us more frequently during our analysis of value and that will offer the answer to many questions. The fact is that our value judgment may vary towards one and the same kind of good at the same time and under the same circumstances. It may differ depending on whether we judge merely single units or greater quantities. Our judgment may differ radically not only on the extent of value, as we shall see in the next chapter, but also on its very existence, which interests us here. But no matter how strange these facts may appear at first, they are explained logically from what we just said about the conditions of the origin of value. Value presumes scarcity, worthlessness abundance, in fact, such a great abundance that a loss of a given quantity does not change the surplus to scarcity.

This conclusion indicates that our valuation may change depending on the quantity being valued. In cases of abundance our valuation depends on whether the quantity of goods under consideration is smaller or greater than the unused surplus. If it is smaller, it can be completely replaced from the surplus. Its loss brings no reduction in well-being and therefore is deemed unimportant. But if the quantity of goods being valued is greater than the unused surplus, the situation hovers between surplus and scarcity. Only possession allows abundance. Loss of possession not only negates abundance but also denies some want satisfaction. Possession is thus a condition of certain well-being and, therefore, it is deemed valuable. Our example clearly illustrates the point. A single gallon is valueless for our farmer who needs a daily water supply of 1000 gallons but has 2000. But if someone wants to purchase 1500 gallons, when considered as a unit, such a quantity is valuable. It comprises not only the whole surplus of 1000 gallons that are unimportant to one farmer but also 500 of those 1000 gallons that are needed on his farm. He cannot forego them without suffering a loss in want satisfaction. They are an indispensable condition of well-being.

The objection may be raised that a theory that allows a good to be arbitrarily called valuable or worthless depending on the size of the valuation unit deprives man's value judgment of a constant basis and delivers it to arbitrariness. A good can arbitrarily be called valuable or worthless depending on the size of the valuation unit. This objection is ill-founded. Man cannot arbitrarily choose the valuation unit. But the very circumstances that cause him to value a certain kind of good simultaneously force him to make a value judgment on the quantity. When I buy a horse, it does not occur to me to value a hundred horses or all horses in the world, and then calculate my bid. But I will have to judge the value of *one* horse based upon my unique circumstance. We must always judge a specific economic situation. That we are capable of making different judgments in different situations is not only understandable but also necessary. Let us imagine a miller who is approached simultaneously by two neighbors. One neighbor is asking for permission to take a pitcher of water from his creek. The other neighbor wants to divert all the water from the mill. If the miller were to establish a uniform rule regarding the use of his water by the neighbors, he would act unwisely in one of the two situations. If he deems all water to be equally valuable, he would refuse the taking of a single pitcher. If he deems all water valueless, he would permit, to his great sorrow, the diversion of the whole creek. But in reality our miller will correctly render two different value judgments: he will deem a single pitcher worthless and without further ado permit its removal. But the whole creek is valuable to him, which will cause him to refuse its diversion.

A simple application of our findings now offers an explanation to the apparent contradiction in the value phenomenon of free goods mentioned above. Free goods are available in abundance. All smaller quantities that do not exhaust this abundance are also valueless according to our deliberations and also our daily experience. However, when we judge a large quantity of free goods exceeding the surplus or even all the free goods of a certain kind, it follows from what has been said that we naturally must attach value to the quantity. We do this because man cannot live without air and water. When we think of all breathable air and all potable water or imagine their disappearance, we correctly attach value to the total available quantities.

In real life we mostly face small quantities of free goods and therefore judge them worthless. Only academic discussions, such as the one above, provide the occasion for different conclusions. In real life it is an exception that we must value large quantities of free goods and therefore attach economic value. In a logging community, for instance, a single tree may be a free and worthless good. But if you propose to the townsfolk that the whole forest be cut, they will undoubtedly attach great value and a high price to it.

Now let us consider another example. The city of Vienna must pay considerable sums to owners for the right to pipe several hundred thousand gallons of water from certain mountain waters to the city on a daily basis. Such a case offers practical proof that our deliberations on the economic value of different quantities of free goods is not imagined but comes from real economic life.

Older value theory dealt with our foregoing scenario in an unfortunate manner. It perceived correctly that valuation of a total supply differs essentially from that of single units. But instead of viewing this difference merely as a special application of the same principle, older theorists developed two different kinds of value: an *abstract value* for the type and class of goods, and a *specific value* for specific samples and small quantities in specific situations.[10]

I consider the abstract class value completely fictitious. It does not exist. If economic value is real significance of goods for man, then all existing value is specific.[11] Just because a good belongs to a certain class or category does not entitle it to anything but participation in the category of goods with the same qualities and thus the *capabilities* associated with its kind. Of course, this is not enough to establish significance for human well-being either in the abstract sense or for an "abstract average being." Real significance

[10] *Rau, Volkswirtschaftslehre*, 8th edition, I, para. 62; after him many others.

[11] Already Schäffle, *Ges. System*, 3rd ed., I, p. 171, stated this correctly.

always assumes dependence of human well-being on goods which must be scarce. This factor, however, is never the characteristic of a category, but always results from a specific situation in which the supply is "scarce." For instance, I cannot say anything about "drinking water" in general except that it has the capability to quench thirst. Even the "abstract average man" can only determine whether a real thirst has been quenched when he has or lacks an abundance of drinking water. The situation determines whether some water has significance for man. Therefore, it is an inadmissible generalization that all drinking water has significance and value. It is true, in a certain sense drinking water in general is valuable: when we think of all the water in the world or, at least, of all the available potable water. But it must be noted that "all the water" and "all the available potable water" constitute specific quantities that owe their value not only to the qualities of water but also to the fact that man cannot live without them.

This leads us to two conclusions: First, the value of a category of goods in their entirety is a specific value. And second, it is not permissible to impute the total value of all the units of a category as a whole to every individual unit. But this is the very error committed by the theory of abstract value, having been led astray apparently by the ambiguity of the term "the whole category." When we say "water has value" we may mean either that all water together is valuable or that every drop of water is valuable. The statement in the first sense is correct. But failure to distinguish it from the second sense led to the error of ascribing "abstract category value" to all water.

Some naïve followers of abstract category value seem to admit in occasional remarks that their definition of value is not for true value. Professor Wagner, for instance, contends that a value judgment giving rise to abstract value "does not necessarily stimulate the desire to retain or acquire a good."[12] He thereby tacitly admits that category value is not affected by a well-being valuation and the category value derived from category

---

[12] *Grundlegung*, 2nd ed., p. 52. To be fully correct, this remark by a prominent scholar should have gone a little further. I am convinced that the precepts upon which abstract category value is built are not only unnecessary, but they also fail to evoke human action when considered by themselves.

membership is nothing but another name for utility. In short, the only significance goods derived from their kind is the utility peculiar to that kind.

At this point, the question arises as to the suitability of using the term "abstract category value." Cogent reasons recommend against its continued use. "Abstract category value" is superfluous as a synonym for utility; as a competitor for a name, it is ambiguous, disturbing, and misleading. Let us therefore reject its use especially since it is unknown in popular language and only known in scientific language as a contrived and pedantic expression.

II
THE MEASURE OF VALUE

The main task of the value theory is the search for the principle that governs value. Its primary problem stems from a peculiar combination of circumstances. On the one hand the correct principle is nearly self-evident. If value is the importance of goods hold for human well-being and if this importance stems from the fact that an improvement in well-being depends on their presence, then it is also clear that the scope of value placed on that good depends on the effect on well-being that the good has. Value is high, if great well-being depends on the good, and it is low, if only negligible well-being is attributed to the good.

There are certain facts in economic life that seem to deny this rather simple and natural explanation. Everyone knows that in economic reality precious stones have a high value, bread and iron a moderate value, air and water usually none at all. Everyone knows that we cannot exist without air to breathe and water to drink, that bread and iron render important welfare services while precious stones mainly serve ornamental wants that play only a very minor role in human welfare. Therefore, whoever advances the principle that the magnitude of value is determined by the importance of a good's welfare services should expect a low value for precious stones, a higher one for bread and iron, and the highest value for water and air. Reality, however, manifests the opposite.

This surprising phenomenon has become a stumbling block for the value theory. Greatest utility and yet smallest value: what a strange contradiction! It is true, the situation was not fully understood and not accurately described due to the confusion of utility with "use value." While high "use value" was incorrectly ascribed to iron and low value to diamonds it was difficult to understand why the "exchange value" of these goods differed so greatly. Of course, there was no shortage of attempts at bridging this glaring gap with contorted explanations.[1] But they failed, which explains why, from Adam Smith to modern times, numerous theorists completely despaired about the connection between human well-being and the nature and measure of value. They resorted to strange, often incoherent explanations: from labor or labor time to costs of production, resistance of nature to man, and other unimaginable things. But because they could not overcome the feeling that the well-being effect had some bearing on value, they described the apparent disagreement of utility and value as a mysterious contradiction, a "contradiction économique."

The following pages show that the older theory unnecessarily abandoned the most natural explanation. *The measure of dependent utility is also the measure of value.* To prove this sentence we merely need to analyze carefully and with casuistic precision the well-being effect that actually depends on a good in any given situation. I am emphasizing the casuistic precision i.e. the practice of applying general principles of correct behavior to specific circumstances and then altering the circumstances slightly to study the effect on the outcome. In fact, the whole study of subjective value is basically an exercise in casuistry i.e. when, under what conditions, and how much well-being depends on a good. It is remarkable that the common man continually and with certainty makes casuistic decisions of this kind in everyday life. He may err occasionally on a relative basic, but never on principal. It is true, he may ascribe a low value to a diamond which he mistakes for a glass pearl. But the basic reflection that human life depends on drinking water will not mislead him to conclude that every gallon of water from his well is a good of incalculable value, worthy of a price of a thousand dollars. It is our task to reflect on the casuistic decisions of life and clarify the rules which the common man applies with

---

[1] The most remarkable attempt of this kind was made by Professor Hildebrand, *Nationalökonomie Gegenwart und Zukunft*, Frankfort, 1848, p. 318 et seq. He believes that at first every goods category receives its total value "according to the sum and rank of human wants they satisfy." This total value then is distributed to all the units of the category. The total value represents the dividend, the number of units the divisor, and the unit value the quotient. Of course, the quotient is all the smaller the greater the divisor, which explains the remarkably small value of units of the most useful but plentiful categories.

such certainty.

A gain of well-being that may depend on an economic good usually consists of want satisfaction. Some apparent exceptions will be discussed later. The right casuistic decision on how much individual well-being depends on a good follows from the answer to two questions: (1) *which want depends on a good*; and (2) *how important is the dependent want or its satisfaction*?

Let us begin with the second question.

It is well known that our wants differ greatly in importance. We tend to rank them by the consequences their lack of fulfillment has upon our well-being. We ascribe the highest importance to those needs the lack of fulfillment of which causes our death. We rank next those needs whose neglect would have permanent ill-effects on our health, our honor, our happiness. Somewhat lower in our ranking are those needs that involve more passing suffering, pain or deprivation. And at the bottom of our list are those wants for which we are merely inconvenienced when we do not satisfy them. We may formulate an importance scale of wants along these lines. However, the scale will differ from individual to individual and even with the same individual at different times. These differences arise from differences in physical and intellectual talent, in education, etc., and cause great differences in wants and needs. Of course, every practical man had better know his own scale if he is to make an intelligent choice for his limited means. Many theorists have felt called upon to develop a scale from the "objective" standpoint of nonpartial scientific consideration.

Everything would be fine and proper if the expression "scale of wants" were not so ambiguous. It can be interpreted to mean either a scale of *categories of wants* or one of specific *wants*, individual wants. If we rank the want categories in entirety according to their significance for human well-being, we undoubtedly ascribe highest rank to our need for food, nearly as high a rank to our need for clothing and lodging, a much lower rank to our wants of tobacco, alcoholic beverages, musical enjoyment, and an even lower rank to our wants of jewelry, etc.

The scale of specific wants looks quite different. Individual wants may differ within one and the same category. Not every hunger sensation is the same, and not every gratification is of equal importance. For instance, the concrete need for food of a man who did not have a bite for eight days and is close to starvation is greater by far than that of a man who has just consumed two courses and is now awaiting the third. The scale of specific wants thus looks quite different and offers many variations. On the scale of categories the want of food preceeds without doubt that of tobacco, alcohol, and jewelry. On the scale of specific wants the different categories frequently overlap. It is true, the most urgent specific wants of the most important categories outrank all others. But their less important wants are frequently outranked by specific wants of lower ranking categories; the last of the important categories may even be topped by the peaks of the lowest category. This is like ranking the ridges of the Rocky Mountains, the Alps and the Pyrenees, and then individual summits of the ridges. In a comparison of ridges the Rocky Mountains rank higher than the Alps and Pyrenees. But when we compare the summits, many Rocky Mountain peaks are overshadowed by some of the Alps or even a few of the Pyrenees.

Thus the question arises, by which scale are we to measure the importance of our wants: by the scale of categories or that of specific wants? This is no superfluous question. We arrive at totally different valuations depending on the choice of scale. If we are to value food, let us say a loaf of bread, and we apply the scale of categories, we find that food occupies a single rank, the highest. And therefore we should assign a fixed value, in fact, the highest value to the loaf of bread. On the other hand, if we apply the scale of specific wants, that of food occupies a variety of ranks. We may ascribe either high, medium, or even very low value.

When put to the test, the older theory chose the wrong approach. It chose the scale of categories. And because the want of food occupies the highest rank and that of jewelry a lower rank, it concluded that bread in general has a high "use value," and jewelry a low one. But it was greatly surprised that in real life the importance of both categories was quite different.

The approach is flawed. The casuist knows that a single slice of bread can satisfy this or that specific hunger sensation at any given time but it cannot satisfy all real and possible present and future sensations. Therefore, it is obviously improper to measure the importance of the slice's effect by the importance of the category. This would be like ascribing the general elevation of the Alps to the height of the Kahlenberg, an unimportant spur near Vienna. In reality, it would not occur to us to honor every slice of bread in our possession as a life-saving treasure, and to rejoice about a loaf of bread bought for a few pennies as if our lives were saved. And we would hardly rebuke someone for jeopardizing our lives, if he should carelessly give away a slice, or waste it, or feed it to an animal. On the other hand, under the older theory, we would have to value the slice in such manner, if the importance of the category food, on which our lives depend, were to be imputed to specific goods.

It is obvious that valuation of specific goods is unrelated to the scale of want categories; it follows the scale of specific wants. To more fully utilize this knowledge let us clearly illustrate and elaborate several points regarding the ranking process or scalation. When I am hungry I do not face the alternative of either satisfying my hunger completely or going hungry, but I may merely reduce my hunger with some food. I may want to eat more later or just forego complete gratification. Naturally, partial gratification has a lesser significance for me than one that is complete. This fact alone is capable of creating the phenomenon mentioned above, that there are specific wants of different importance within each and every category.

Another remarkable circumstance follows from this fact. It is common to find that the same gratification continually repeated gives less enjoyment from a certain point on until it finally turns into a pain, dissatisfaction, or aversion. Everyone can experience that appetite for a fourth or fifth course is less satisfying than the first, and when more and more courses are served the joy of eating turns into disgust. The same may happen with prolonged concerts, lectures, walks, plays, and any other physical and intellectual pleasures.

Let us put this into our technical language: specific partial wants, in which our want sensations can be divided, and the successive partial gratifications that can be attained with equal quantities of goods usually have unequal significance that *gradually declines to zero*.

This explains a great number of assertions made above. First, it explains that within one and the same want category there can be specific wants or partial wants of different importance. In fact, there not only *can* be but also *must* be specific or partial wants for all divisible wants (which comprise the vast majority of wants). In particular, it explains that even in the most important want categories there are lower and lowest ranks of significance. The more important categories differ from the less important ones only as, so-to-speak, their tops rise above all others while their bottoms are on equal level with the others.

And finally, it also explains that it not only *can* happen occasionally, as stated above, that a specific want of a very important category is surpassed by a specific want of a less significant category, but that it is also a quite normal and natural phenomenon. At any time there are countless specific food wants that are weaker and less important than many a specific want of quite unimportant categories, such as wants of jewelry, dancing, tobacco, singing birds, etc.

Let us try to present the scalation of our wants in a table. Based on prior conclusions, the table looks as shown on the following page:[2]

[2] Cf. Menger, *ibid.*, p. 93.

I	II	III	IV	V	VI	VII	VIII	IX	X
10									
9	9								
8	8	8							
7	7	7	7						
6	6	6		6					
5	5	5		5	5				
4	4	4	4	4	4	4			
3	3	3		3	3		3		
2	2	2		2	2		2	2	
1	1	1	1	1	1		1	1	1
0	0	0	0	0	0	0	0	0	0

In this table, the Roman numerals I to X denote the different want categories and their rank in descending order. I represents the most important category, for instance, the need for food; V a category of medium importance, for instance, the want of alcoholic beverages; and X the lowest imaginable category. The Arabic numerals 10 to 1 denote the specific wants and partial wants within the various categories. They also denote ranking with 10 indicating the highest possible specific want, 9 the next important one, and 1 the least important want.

The table illustrates that the more important the category the greater is its most important specific want. But there are also all the other lower ranks down to the last. The only exceptions are categories IV and VII in which some wants of the descending order are lacking. They represent rather rare wants the successive satisfaction of which is either unsatisfactory or impossible. Such a want must be satisfied completely or not at all. The want for a space heater, for instance, is completely satisfied by a single heater so that no other is needed.

And finally, the table reveals that in the most important category I there are specific wants of the lowest degree 1 while in nearly all lower ranking categories there are specific wants of higher degree.

Many goods are capable of fulfilling the wants of several

different want categories. For instance, rye can be used as food, as the base to make whisky, and as feed for animals. Of course, such goods face a corresponding increase in the number of specific wants whose importance may bear on that good's ultimate valuation. For rye, for instance, the complete category I (specific wants for food) combines with the specific wants for whisky (category V), etc. An exchange economy generalizes and strengthens this valuation process. Exchange allows exchanging a quantity of one good to satisfy the wants of other categories. We shall make important use of this fact for the explanation of value phenomena later in the text[3]. At this point I merely want to consider the nature and ranking of those specific wants that can flow from a specific good.

Let us also consider the question: *which among several of many wants depends on a single good?*

This question could not arise if economic life were so simple as to allow only single wants and goods to confront each other. A good may be capable of satisfying a single specific want and also be the only available unit of its kind. In such a case it is clear that satisfaction of the single want depends completely on the availability of the single good. But in real life the case is seldom so simple. It is usually complicated in two ways. One and the same good usually can satisfy different specific wants each having different degrees of importance. This is especially so when several units are available. It is up to us to decide which unit we apply to the satisfaction of an important want and which to an unimportant one. A very simple example: on a hunt I carry two equal loaves of bread. I need one for my own gratification, the other for my dog's gratification. It is obvious that my own nourishment is much more important to me than that of my dog. And it is equally obvious that it is left to me to decide which one I will consume and which one I shall give to my dog. And now the question arises, which of the two wants is dependent on my bread?

One might be tempted to answer: that want for which each loaf

---

[3] In this section I do not plan to discuss exchange phenomena, which shall be reserved for the second part, "The Theory of Objective Exchange Value." But wherever the possibility of exchange exerts its influence on the subjective value of goods I must treat it as a given fact as does the theory of subjective value.

was intended. But it can be seen immediately that this decision would be wrong. Such a conclusion would suggest that both loaves being meant for the satisfaction of wants of different importance also would have to have different values. On the other hand, don't two equal goods available in the same situation have to be of equal value?

Again a simple casuistic deliberation points the way. We can find the dependent want by determining which want would not be satisfied in absence of the good. As can readily be seen, it would not be the want which the owner chose by flipping a coin. It would be the *least important of all possible wants*, in fact, of all those wants that would be covered by the total supply.

Serious consideration of his own well-being leads every intelligent man to maintain a certain constant order in his want satisfaction. No one is so foolish as to deplete his supplies in the satisfaction of unimportant wants, and then go without the essentials. Everyone means to cover first the most important wants, followed by those of lesser importance, so that the wants of a lower degree are met only when all other wants of a higher degree have been met. Man stays faithful to this rule of reason even when the given supply is reduced by one unit. Of course, the previous plans must be reconsidered in light of the reduced quantity. No longer can all wants be satisfied. Naturally, intelligent man endeavors to shift the loss to the least sensitive area, that is, if the loss happens to affect a good meant for important employment, he will not forego this satisfaction and stubbornly cling to his old plan to satisfy unimportant wants. But he will instead satisfy the more important want and withdraw the want which ranked lowest among all previous wants. In our example, no one will face starvation when he loses the loaf meant for his own consumption by nevertheless feeding the second loaf to his dog. But everyone will quickly change his plan, assign the remaining loaf its more important function and shift the loss to the less important rank, i.e. feeding the dog.

To summarize: all wants that are more important than the last (marginal) one are not affected by the loss. Their satisfaction remains assured through substitution. Equally unaffected are those wants that are less important than the last one, for they remain unsatisfied with or without the good. Only the last of the otherwise satisfied wants is affected; it is satisfied if the good is available and remains unsatisfied without it. It is the sought-after dependent want.

We have now arrived at the heart of our investigation. *The value of a good is determined by the importance of that specific want or partial want that is least important among all those wants that are met by the good's supply.*[4] It is not the greatest utility a good may afford that determines its value, nor is it the average utility, but rather the smallest utility or the marginal use, which the good may rationally afford in a given situation. To save ourselves time, in the name of expediency[5] let us, like Wieser,[6] call this least important utility the economic *marginal utility* of the good. The law of good's value can thus be stated in its simplest terms: *the value of a good is determined by its marginal utility.*

This sentence is the foundation of our value theory. All that follows depends on it and is derived from it. The sentence also clearly points up the conflict between our theory and the older one. When the older theory attributed value to utility, it ofttimes used a good's highest utility or the medium average utility as the yardstick for value. It recognized the highest utility by assigning the full rank of its category to every unit. And with Hildebrand[7] it recognized average utility by adding the sum and rank of all wants of a category and then dividing it by the number of available goods. In contrast, we attribute value to the lowest point on the scale of utility. "The lowest point on the scale of utility is the starting point

---

[4] This includes the goods of another category suited for substitution. This is an addition that merely has casuistic significance, with which I do not want to burden our basic investigation. For further particulars see below.

[5] Cf. preceding note.

[6] *Über den Ursprung und die Hauptgesetze des wirtschaftlichen Wertes*, p. 128. Jevons uses the term "final degree of utility" and "terminal utility." Professor Menger, who first and with full clarity developed these principles, still lacks the ease of a short technical term. He expresses the principle as follows (ibid., p. 98 et seq): "In every specific case, only those want satisfactions covered by the total goods supply depend on the possession of a certain available part-quantity that has the smallest significance for an individual. To him, the value of a part-quantity of available goods equals the significance of the least important want satisfaction that is covered by the total quantity and obtained by an equal part-quantity."

[7] See footnote above, p. 24

for value."[8] At this point, it may be not only advisable but even mandatory to submit one more proof of our basic principle. So far we have offered proof only through abstract deductions; now let us also prove our principle with real life examples.[9] At first a simple concrete example.

A settler whose hut lies deep in the forest far removed from civilization just harvested five sacks of grain. They must last until the next harvest. Because he is an orderly and thoughtful man, he makes plans for the sacks' intended uses. He absolutely needs one sack for his survival. A second sack preserves his health and strength. Because there is a limit to how much rye he can enjoy, he decides to add meat to his diet; the third sack is assigned to feed some poultry. The fourth sack is used to make whisky. And after his modest needs are thus met, he decides to use the last sack to feed a number of parrots whose company he enjoys. Of course, all these uses are not equally important. Let us use a scale from one to ten to illustrate the case in numerical form. Our settler assigns the highest rank 10 to his survival, 8 to that of his health, and in descending order, 6 to the improvement of his diet through the addition of meat, 4 to the enjoyment of whisky and, finally, the lowest possible rank 1 to the feeding of parrots. And now let us put ourselves in the place of the settler and ask the question: under these circumstances what significance does *one* sack of rye possess for his well-being?

As we know, this can be shown by considering what happens if one sack is lost. We would not be very smart, if we were to deprive ourselves of our meals and thus lose our lives and health while making whisky and feeding chickens and parrots. Sound deliberation leads us to only one solution, we will cover the most important wants with the remaining four sacks. We will forego only the last, the "marginal utility." This is the enjoyment of parrots.

---

[8] Wieser, *ibid.*, p. 129.

[9] I would not belabor this point and I would certainly have kept the preceding analysis much shorter, if it were not for the confusion displayed by several eminent authors who opposed my predecessors and the theory of marginal utility (Especially Schäffle and H. Dietzel). They convinced me that the foundation of our theory cannot be presented too clearly and distinctly in order to avoid misunderstandings.

The well-being that depends on the fifth sack of rye is merely the pleasure of parrots. We thus value a single sack by the least significant utility. In fact, we value every *single* sack. If all sacks are equal it makes no difference to us whether we lose sack A or B--provided four sacks remain to cover our more important wants. Let us vary the example. Let us assume that under similar conditions we own only three sacks. How much is one sack worth now? The test again is quite simple. With three sacks we can satisfy only the three most important wants. With two sacks we must limit ourselves to the satisfaction of two wants and forego the third want, poultry. Possession of the third sack, which could be any one of the three sacks, allows satisfaction of the third important want, which is the last want covered by our supply. Any valuation other than that of marginal utility would obviously conflict with reality; it would be specious.

Let us assume, finally, that under similar conditions we possess only one sack of rye. It should be obvious that we will forego all other enjoyments and employ this sole sack towards our survival for which it barely suffices. And it is equally clear that the loss of this single sack would jeopardize our lives. Its possession means life, its loss death. In accordance with our principle of marginal utility, the last sack of rye has the greatest significance for our well-being. The highest utility, the preservation of life, is the only and last, the "marginal utility."

Let us now extend our test beyond imaginary examples to real experiences of economic life. We frequently find that the quantity of goods varies inversely to their value. The greater the supply of a category, the smaller tends to be the value of a single unit, and vice versa. It is well known that this principle is the basis for the law of "demand and supply." But it goes beyond exchange and price. A collector, for instance, values a single unit that represents a certain class in his collection much more highly than one of a dozen equal units. It can be demonstrated easily that these facts, verified by common experience, follow our theory of marginal utility. In fact, the greater the supply of certain goods, the greater can be the satisfaction of wants that are dependent upon them. And the less important wants are the last ones to be satisfied. Of course, their satisfaction would be jeopardized by the loss of a single unit. In short, the greater the supply of goods, the lower is the marginal utility that determines their value. If goods are in such abundance that some units remain after complete satisfaction of all dependent wants, i.e., if some units remain without useful employment, then the marginal utility must be zero. And a single remaining unit of the respective category lacks any value.

This leads us to a natural explanation of a phenomenon that was so surprising at first. Less useful goods, such as pearls and diamonds, evidence such high values, while more useful goods, such as bread and iron, have lower values, and water and air have none at all. The fact is that pearls and diamonds are available in such small quantities that our wants for them are only partially gratified, and the marginal utility that is reached by their satisfaction is relatively high. But fortunately bread and iron, water and air, are usually available in such large quantities[10] that satisfaction of all important wants is assured, and possession of a single unit or specific part-unit assures satisfaction of all remaining wants. Under abnormal conditions such as a city being held under siege or a trip through a desert, water and bread could become scarce. Should this happen the smaller supply suffices merely for gratification of the most important specific wants. The marginal utility quickly climbs and, according to our principle, so does the value of the goods we value so lowly under normal conditions. This is verified by the evidence that people are willing to pay such enormous prices in these situations for simple foods.[11] Thus, this scenario, which upon first glance appeared to contradict our theory, indeed offers splendid proof and verification of its validity. Furthermore, I need not emphasize the invalidity of the theory of category value or of Hildebrand's average value in an explanation of value.

I leave it to the reader to test further the correctness of our principle. It will pass the test. In fact, I am convinced that it is

[10] Especially for rich people who buy pearls and diamonds.

[11] It could be objected that these high prices surely indicate only higher "exchange value" while the subjective use value may have remained unchanged. We reply that bidding or asking a high price already presumes a high subjective valuation of the good, while the willingness with which we usually may give away a good, for instance, drinking water, clearly indicates that even from a subjective point of view we do not regard highly the thing we give away so freely.

corroborated both by logic and experience. I would even dare to maintain that only misunderstandings can give rise to doubt.[12] Therefore I feel justified in my hope that the theory of marginal utility will soon find common usage in our science and become the foundation and keystone for further attempts at refining the long debated value theory.

It is appropriate now to add a few remarks which I intentionally avoided lest I delay our main investigation. They concern all casuistic situations where the principle of marginal utility is applied and how this, in turn, affects our appraisal of value. They may be significant for practical reasons.

The general principle that affects our consideration of marginal utility is very simple. But we must be very careful in an analysis of the particular situation of the individual who makes the value judgment. At times we add a good to our supply and wonder about the additional want satisfaction. At other times we subtract the good from a given supply and ponder about the satisfaction that is still covered. This means that a certain layer of wants, i.e. its lowest layer, has lost its supply: the lowest layer reveals the marginal utility that determines the valuation.[13] Of course the scope of this

---

[12] Schäffle's recent objection published on the occasion of the publication of Wieser's work *Über den Ursprung und die Hauptgesetze des wirtschaftlichen Wertes* seems to rest on a misunderstanding of the theory he opposes. (*Zeitschrift für die gesamte Staatswissenschaft*. 1885, p. 451 et seq.) For further details see below p. 39.

[13] On two occasions we feel called upon to make value judgments. First, when we are concerned with relinquishing a good from our possession, for instance, to give it away, exchange it, or consume it. Second, when we are concerned with acquiring a good. In the two cases of valuation our trains of thought differ somewhat. The good we already possess is valued for the loss that we suffer without it, thus for the last covered gratification. The good we do not yet possess is valued inversely for the addition of utility which its acquisition assures us, that is, for the most important gratification among those that remained unsatisfied with the previous supply. Of course, both methods lead to the same result: the last want satisfaction that is assured by the good is always identical to the first satisfaction without the good. In our text I chose a formulation that is general enough to encompass both methods. Many a reader may have misgivings that an analysis of marginal utility, as described previously, is quite cumbersome and that they are unaware of its application in their daily valuations. I merely would like to mention here that in practical analyses we use many abbreviations

(continued...)

layer may differ greatly according to the quality of the object. If it is a single unit of a consumers' good, for instance food, the marginal utility usually reflects only a single specific want or merely a partial want. On the other hand, if we are to appraise a durable good that is capable of repeated use, or if we appraise a large quantity of goods as a single unit, it is natural then that a large sum of specific wants falls in the dependent layer. Possession or non-possession of a piano, for instance, offers hundreds of musical enjoyments, possession of ten bottles of wine affects hundreds of taste enjoyments the significance of which must be addressed in our value judgment.

In such cases a phenomenon may appear to be very strange at first, but upon closer investigation it is easily explained. It may be that the valuation of a large quantity of goods does not coincide with that of a single unit. In fact, the larger quantity may be worth many times more than the smaller quantity. Five sacks of grain, for instance, may have ten times or 100 times more value than one sack. This is always the case if the larger quantity, when received as a unit, comprises a large part of the total supply and its loss would cause a serious reduction of one's satisfaction. This principle also applies when the loss of the larger quantity deprives those specific wants which are considerably more important than the marginal or lowest want. Of course, the lowest want level that can be satisfied by the larger quantity is comprised of specific wants of unequal intensity and different importance. It requires only a simple mathematical calculation to show that the sum of a number of unequal factors must be greater than the product of the last, the smallest factor times the number of factors. 5 + 4 + 3 + 2 + 1 is always greater than 5 x 1.

Let us return for further illustration to our example of the settler. Remember that he owned five sacks of grain and a single sack of rye was worth the enjoyment of parrots. All five sacks together, however, determine not only the sum of satisfactions of which each one equals the enjoyment of parrots, but they include the enjoyment of parrots plus the enjoyment of whisky, plus the

---

[13] (...continued)
and recollections and require much less time than for our theoretical presentation. I shall return to this objection later.

poultry meat, plus preservation of health, plus preservation of life. The sum is not five times as great as the pleasure of parrots, but infinitely greater. When placed in the position of our pioneer, every reader would agree that he would be willing to sell one of the five sacks at a modest price, let us say $5, but that he would not sell five sacks for $25, in fact he would not sell them at any price.

In everyday life, we seldom have the opportunity to observe this casuistic peculiarity. In our system of division of labor, business sales are usually made from a surplus that is not intended for the satisfaction of the owners' personal wants. When a sugar producer sells 100 pounds of sugar or even a ton, the gratification of his personal wants of sugar remains unaffected. In this case a ton of sugar is worth only 20 times the hundredweight of sugar. But the principle described above is felt as soon as only personal supplies are involved. For instance, he who only possesses two copies of a book of a copperplate engraving or an old coin, etc. demands more than twice the price for both than he would ask for one only.

This peculiarity is most keenly felt, if a good's quantity viewed as a unit comprises the total available supply of goods. Our value judgment of such totals will always be extraordinarily high even if a single unit has a low value or, in the case of free goods, has no value at all. In short, the totality of all goods affects the satisfaction of all dependent wants, including the most important specific wants. There cannot be any doubt, for instance, that the total supply of water available to a city is very valuable because without it the inhabitants would die from thirst. Of course, a single gallon of water can nevertheless be valueless, and ofttimes is.

Those who overlook the casuistic difference between the value of the total and that of single units can easily go astray. As mentioned above, it is this difference that is the foundation of "abstract category value." Its advocates recognize quite correctly that the totality of free goods of a certain category, as for instance all existing water, or the atmosphere air, has high value for mankind. But then they concluded incorrectly that every unit must be valuable thanks to its membership in the valuable category. And they named this value the "abstract category value" in contrast to the genuine concrete value. The truth is that a single unit has no value at all, but the whole category a normal concrete value. The abstract category value is a creation of imagination without any reality.

Unfortunately, it was this same concept that led to a position recently taken by Schäffle in a critical analysis of the theory of marginal utility.[14] He objects to the conclusion that a desert traveler values his water supply according to the relatively small marginal utility which the last expendable drop of water provides for cooking and washing. According to Schäffle, "the fear of thirst will affect his attitude towards the whole supply." And this fear will cause him "to secure a good safety cap, to treat the bottle carefully, to prevent its over-heating, etc." Quite correct! When the water supply is considered as total, not only the needs for washing and cooking but also that of thirst will have a bearing on valuation. In Schäffle's example, it is the total supply of water that one must consider. If the bottle has a hole, it cannot be known whether only the relatively expendable part meant for cooking and washing will leak out or whether *all* the water will be lost. But Schäffle is mistaken if he deduces any argument against the theory of marginal utility from this scenario. For he only refutes what the marginal utility theory does not contend at all: namely, that the value of the total is determined by the marginal utility of the last unit contained in the total. On the contrary, our theory emphasizes specifically that it is equally incorrect to judge the value of a part according to the utility of the total as it is to judge the value of the total according to the utility of its parts.

Our theory merely contends that every good and every quantity of goods receives its value from the corresponding marginal utility, i.e. from the smallest utility that can economically be obtained from it or its substitute. And this is true in spite of the stated objections. It is undeniable that any quantity of the water supply, for example each quart, is valued according to the marginal utility of the last quantity meant for washing and cooking. Professor Schäffle's own assumption that some water will be used for cooking and washing provides the best proof. If "fear of thirst" does not prevent such unimportant uses, it cannot possibly impute a value that is higher than the importance of the less important uses. Moreover, the high value ascribed to the whole water supply is consistent with the theory of marginal utility. When seen as a closed unit, the water

---

[14] *Tübinger Zeitschrift*, 1885, p. 451 *et seq*; cf. above p. 36.

supply is the only, the first, and last available unit of its kind. Therefore, the total utility, which includes the preservation of his life, coincides with the utility of the last unit, that is, with the relevant marginal utility.

Mr. Schäffle, nevertheless, seems to believe that the high value of the total supply discredits the marginal utility theory. In my belief, his error flows from a failure to separate the concepts "every single part-unit of the supply" and "the whole supply." And then he imputes his error to the theory he attacks.[15]

Let us turn to another point. Our analysis reveals that the marginal utility that determines the value of a good is not the same as the utility the good provides.[16] For it is usually another utility, the utility of the last unit or the last equal part-unit that can be substituted that determines the value of a good. Under simple conditions this utility, although being that of another good, is at least that of a good of the same category. In our example, the value of every unit, for instance, of the first sack of rye, is determined by the utility of another, the last sack, which is still the utility of a sack of rye. In an advanced exchange economy, however, the situation can be much more complicated. It is possible to exchange the goods of one category for those of another, which, in turn, makes it possible to shift the loss in one category to another. We need not replace the loss of a unit with another unit of the same category. But we may use goods from another category and cover the loss through exchange. Thus the loss of a good of a certain category actually means the loss of the utility which the substituting goods of another category would otherwise have provided. And because

---

[15] In the text we only considered the case in which the value of a large entity is valued much higher than its units. In concrete situations the very opposite may occur and the large entity may be valued incomparably low. This may happen when we are concerned with the acquisition of goods quantities rather than with relinquishing them. For instance, if our settler possesses no grain at all, then the acquisition of a first sack means preservation of life for him. The acquisition of each additional sack means correspondingly less and, therefore, purchase of the fifth sack much less than five times the value of the first sack. $5 + 4 + 3 + 2 + 1$ is less than 5×5. In practical life the attentive reader can observe numerous cases of this kind, which are readily explained by our theory.

[16] This applies either to single units or those units that happen to be chosen for the least important service.

the latter may not be taken from the most important uses but rather from the least significant ones, the loss affects the margin of utility of the substituted goods. The marginal utility and value of a good is thus determined by the marginal utility of the substituted quantity of another category.

An example. I have a single winter coat. It is stolen. Immediate replacement with another coat is out of the question because I only had one coat. Nor am I inclined to suffer the loss at the place where it occurred. The need for winter clothing is rather urgent because its loss may adversely affect my health and perhaps even my life. Therefore, I shall try to shift the loss to another goods category. I shall buy a new coat in exchange for goods that otherwise would have found different employment. Of course, I withdraw the substituted goods from those employments that are least important to me, that is, from the "marginal utility." If I am well-to-do, I probably will take $100, which the new winter coat may cost, from my wallet and then forego some luxury expenditures. If I am neither so affluent nor really poor, the loss of cash will have to be made up through various savings in my monthly expenditures. But if I should be poor, lacking the necessary cash and being unable to save it out of my monthly income, I must sell or pawn some expendable assets. And finally, if I should be so poverty-stricken that I can satisfy only the most important specific wants from all these categories, I will not be able to shift the loss to other want categories. I must get along without a winter coat as well as I can.

Let us carefully analyze the situation of the stolen coat. The question of how much well-being depends on the possession or lack of the winter coat must be viewed as follows: for the well-to-do it is a luxury expenditure, for the middle-class person, it requires a small saving in the household budget, for the poor person there is a loss of the utility of an item sold or pawned, and for the poverty-stricken person the loss of the coat means the loss of effective protection for his health. Only for the last person is the value of the coat determined by the immediate marginal utility of its own category. In the three other situations the value of the coat is determined by the marginal utility of substituted goods and want categories.[17]

This casuistic analysis is very important in our highly developed exchange economy. I believe that the majority of objective valuations occurs as described above. In fact, we rarely value goods for their direct utility but nearly always for the "substitution utility" of other goods. But I would like to emphasize that even in a market economy we do not *always* apply this valuation method. We only do this if the marginal utility of the substituted goods is smaller than the direct marginal utility of its own category. To be more precise, we use this method, if prices and supply conditions of the relatively more important wants must be foregone when the loss is covered by goods of its own categories rather than when the purchase price of the substituted unit is pulled from other wants. Only the smallest utility that directly or indirectly depends on a good determines the true marginal utility and value.

Similar complications can arise where replacement goods can quickly be made through production. Complications of this kind are rather important for the value theory because they offer insight into the influence production costs have on value. Therefore, they require special attention which we will address in more detail below. At this point, however, we would like to interrupt our casuistic digression and return to the main task.

So far we have explained value with marginal utility as our starting point. But we can pursue this notion a little further by raising the question: what are the circumstances that determine the extent of marginal utility?

Now we must consider the relationship of demand and supply. Having frequently touched upon the manner in which these two factors affect the degree of marginal utility, I shall forego a detailed explanation and merely present a short formula: marginal utility is determined by the intensity of demand. In other words, the greater the importance of the want seeking satisfaction and the smaller the quantity of available goods the higher is also the intensity of wants

---

[17] Wieser's sentence that the marginal utility "must always belong to the utility sphere of the same goods category" is valid only with the reservation stated right there (*ibid.*, p. 128).

that forego satisfaction. Inversely, the lower and less urgent the wants that await satisfaction and the greater the supply of available goods, the lower are also want satisfaction, marginal utility, and value. Stated differently although less precisely, *utility* and *scarcity* are the prerequisites for or sources of value. As the given utility of a good reveals its ability to satisfy more or less important wants, so does its rank offer a measure of the degree of marginal utility. But scarcity determines the extent to which marginal utility can rise in a specific case.

The possibility of exchange again leads to complications. At any time exchange facilitates the substitution of a given want category at the expense of another category. And once again the relevant marginal utility is shifted from the category under valuation to that of the substituted good. The resulting complications are as follows. Factors that exert an influence are, first, the ratio of demand and supply that exists relative to all marketable goods throughout an economy. This ratio affects, as shall be shown in part two of this book, the prices that must be paid for the substituted unit, and thereby the extent of loss suffered by those goods categories from which the substituted good is drawn. And secondly, influence is exerted by the individual's ratio of demand and supply in his want categories from which the substitution is drawn. In other words, it is his choice of substituted good that determines whether the loss affects a high or low level of want satisfaction and whether a small or large marginal utility must be foregone.[18]

The doctrine that the extent of marginal utility is determined by the ratios of demand and supply bears many applications and practical consequences that may be analyzed in a detailed value theory. At this point I only want to emphasize two consequences

---

[18] For further illustration let us revisit our example of the stolen winter coat. The demand for one coat involves not only the actual possession of one but also its replacement through the purchase of a new one. The marginal utility is shifted to that want category from which the purchase price must be taken. It will be all the greater (1) the more expensive the new winter coat is, which is determined by the ratio of demand and supply for winter coats, and (2) the more poorly the victim's other want categories are covered. Depending on the various supply situations, as already mentioned, the dependent marginal utility may vary between unimportant luxury enjoyment and painful deprivation.

which we shall use later in the theory of objective exchange value. First, as the ratio of demand and supply varies greatly with individuals, one and the same good may have different subjective values with different people. This is a fact without which exchange would not be conceivable. Under identical conditions the same goods have different values for the rich and the poor, smaller values for the rich and greater values for the poor. Because the rich are better endowed in all goods categories their everyday satisfactions revolve around unessential wants. Change in goods satisfaction is therefore less significant. But for poor people who can only satisfy their most important wants, important utility hinges on every single good. In fact, experience shows that poor people deem the acquisition of goods a joyful event and their losses as painful. Rich people, on the other hand, greet such an event with indifference. Compare, if you will, the state of mind of a poor clerk who loses his monthly salary of $300 with that of a millionaire losing the same amount. For the former the loss means painful deprivation for a whole month. For the latter it is nothing more than the loss of some idle luxury expenditure.[19]

Our discussions about value reveal a gap. This does not mean that it is of great importance, but the very existence of such a gap may sow distrust against our theory. Therefore, I would like to return to the beginning of this section for one last short investigation.

We said[20] that the gain of well-being that depends on a good *usually* results from the satisfaction of a want. As far as this rule applies, the law of marginal utility applies, as has already been proven. But we also indicated earlier, this rule has certain exceptions. And it remains to be demonstrated when they exist and how valuation occurs under those circumstances.

The distinction between rule and exception can be clarified as follows. A certain want satisfaction always depends on a good when the supply of goods is limited. Loss of a good not only limits the means of gratification but it also restricts the satisfaction. One

---

[19] This is not to deny that rich people often value the same good more highly relative to money than poor people. To them, money means less than to the poor.

[20] See p. 25.

good more or less also means one satisfied satisfaction more or less. Under exceptional circumstances, however, it is possible that the loss of a good brings about a special substitution fervor that allows us to acquire the needed substitution unit without reduction of our other goods supply. Instead, we are spurred on to exert ourselves beyond our prior level of exertion, thus producing the substitute good which we otherwise would not have had. In such cases, loss of a good does not necessarily cause loss of a want satisfaction as the gap in supply is closed by an extraordinary substitution effort, but it reduces our well-being through imposition of a disutility or inconvenience which we would otherwise have escaped.

An example. Tickets for an interesting celebration, let us say a coronation, are made available without charge, but only upon personal petition. I own such a ticket. If I lose it, I would not need to forego participation in the celebration, but would merely have to call again. Possession of the ticket thus means for me that it saves me the inconvenience and bother of a second personal petition.

This exception requires two conditions: First, there must be an opportunity to acquire a replacement merely at the price of an inconvenience; second, this inconvenience must be smaller than the positive marginal utility of the good. For instance, if I deem the inconvenience of a repeated petition for the ticket to be greater than the positive enjoyment of the celebration, I would forego the coronation. And thus the loss would again affect the positive satisfaction.

In real life, both conditions occur rarely and then mostly affect small and insignificant objects. We often may have the opportunity to make substitutions through voluntary additional labor exertion.[21] This presumes not only leisure time that can be used for voluntary effort, but also an opportunity to render additional services in our leisure time, which is rare for the majority of people. The

[21] Now and then we may use other inconveniences as an excuse to acquire goods. Only the casuist may bother to think of such cases. For instance, in order to harden a boy, his teacher may promise him a desired toy as a reward for the brave voluntary suffering of pain. No matter how unimportant such cases may be in reality, it is important to remember in theory that labor and inconvenience are not the only circumstances on which valuation may be based.

conditions of a labor contract and professional customs are such that our services are rendered mostly in a fixed number of hours per day. We are seldom willing to increase them or, even if we wanted to, may be unable to prolong our work for the sake of a special economic want. In a factory, with eight hour shifts, the shops are seldom kept open for the sake of a single worker who, for a few days, would like to work nine hours in order to replace some broken household goods. The fact is that our professional services mostly yield a certain measure of goods and thus a certain measure of want satisfaction. Loss of this satisfaction does not lead to greater labor exertion but rather loss of want satisfaction. Therefore, it is this same loss which we analyzed above that usually determines the value of economic goods. Without a doubt small efforts are frequently made during our leisure time to acquire some goods we would not purchase with the proceeds of our serious economic labor. For instance, on my walks I like to gather flowers which, when dried and arranged in bouquets, adorn my room. When the flowers wilt I do not lose a single want satisfaction, but merely the effort of gathering, drying, etc., assuming I deem this effort smaller than the positive utility of the flowers.

How do we determines the value in these exceptional cases? The answer is simple. The significance of these goods for our well-being flows from the fact that their possession saves us a disutility or inconvenience. And well-being and value are that much more important the greater the disutility and inconvenience they prevent.

How does this concept relate to the law of marginal utility discussed above? Upon cursory consideration one might conclude that we are proceeding from a different principle than before-there the utility and here disutility or labor. I vehemently reject such an opinion. Our theory explains value always from one and the same principle. It always deduces value from the degree of well-being that depends on the possession of the good. While economic situations are complex and diverse, the welfare effect may exert either as additional positive utility toward want satisfaction or, though much more seldom, as prevention of disutility. As long as we develop the principle in accordance with the realities of life, we will not waver in principle but rather reveal the effect of its application.

We may pursue both principles even further. The salient characteristic of the theory of marginal utility is that it makes the smallest economically feasible benefit the decisive factor for determining value. This characteristic is also evident here. As was demonstrated above, if the disutility prevented by a good is smaller than its positive satisfaction, the true marginal utility of the good is the prevention of disutility. This is connected with the very nature of marginal utility in that it does not depend on a good's own utility but that of its eventual means of substitution. In some cases, substitution can be made within a good's own category; in others, the substitution is shifted to goods of other categories. In still rarer cases, a substitution can be made to some disutility or inconvenience. If we thus explain economic value as the disutility saved, it constitutes no deviation from the principle, but merely a correct application of the law of marginal utility.[22]

---

[22] In his *Grundsätze*, which paved the way for the theory of subjective goods value, Professor Menger merely covered the normal situation, which is a little too narrow. Professor Wieser in his *Ursprung und Hauptgesetze*, p. 104 *et seq*., also covered the exceptions but considered only labor as a determining factor for value and did too little for the theoretical unification of apparent exceptions to the rule with the principle of marginal utility. Before them, von Mangoldt had touched upon the thought (*Volkswirtschaftlehre*, 1868, p. 132 et seq.). But it seems that this sagacious scholar intended to cover all cases in which production costs exert an influence on value (Cf. *ibid*., p. 133). He thus overrated considerably its applicability. I need not emphasize for attentive readers that our discussion reflects neither approval of nor actual cooperation with the so-called labor theory of value as presented by Ricardo, Rodbertus, or Marx. Elsewhere (*History and Critique of Interest Theories*, 1884, p. 428 to 444, English edition, Libertarian Press, 1959, p. 241 - 321) I wrote a detailed critique of that theory. But it is appropriate to elaborate my point of view towards Professor Schäffle's value theory which, in an unusual manner, connects the considerations of utility and sacrifice.

In my opinion, Professor Schäffle has earned an honored place in the history of the value theory because of two achievements: First, he found the characteristic term "significance" for value; and second, he fortunately and sensibly applied the theory of subjective value to the theory of objective exchange value. Unfortunately, the essence of his value theory rests on an unsatisfactory and unclear compromise between two different principles. In his *Gesellschaftliches System*, 3rd ed., 1873, from which I am quoting, Professor Schäffle defines value in general as "the significance or meaning ascribed to a good." (p. 162). As far as *economic* value is concerned, there are "as many aspects of value for economic

(continued...)

[22] (...continued)
action as there are considerations and causes for economic deliberation." As the latter pertains to highest utility and lowest cost, he distinguishes between use value and cost value. "The significance that is ascribed to a certain good at its lowest costs constitutes its cost value; its significance with respect to its highest possible utility is its use value or utility value. In a broad sense of the word, only that good is valuable whose recognized utility at least reaches the perceptible costs. *True economic value is a balance quantity that comprises cost value and use value.*" (p. 166). What Professor Schäffle means by the term "balance" can be deduced from the following sentence: "Economic value becomes greater *the more the use value exceeds cost value.* True value drops to zero if both are equal, and it turns to loss whenever use value falls below cost value." (p. 168). According to Schäffle, the value of a good is determined by the difference between the highest utility a good may afford and the lowest costs at which it can be produced. This sentence cannot at all be defended. It directly contradicts the facts and Schäffle himself repeatedly contradicted it. If a speculator builds a $100,000 apartment house in a poor neighborhood where there is little demand for it, and this apartment house is worth only $50,000 in rent value, does this make its "true" economic value zero or even minus? Certainly not, for a sale probably would realize a positive value of approximately $50,000. Or consider instead a good speculator who builds a $100,000 house at a place at which its use value is $120,000, does this call for a "true" value of only $20,000, which is the difference between $120,000 and $100,000? Certainly not! It will amount to the full $120,000.

Mr. Schäffle himself declares all those goods valueless that are acquired without cost (p. 168, note 1). Quite correct, but contrary to his own principle! Where the cost value is zero, the difference between use value and cost value, which constitutes Mr. Schäffle's "balance," is all the greater and therefore should lead to greater value. Furthermore, Professor Schäffle (p. 178) denies all free goods not only "true economic value," but also use value. Again quite correct, but contrary to his own principle! For the use value merely rests on the "highest possible use" and has nothing to do with cost and deprivation, (both of which are synonymous with Schäffle, for instance, p. 168, notes 4 and 5). The circumstance that "they cost nothing and are missed by no one" cannot deny them use value. Such contradictions give testimony not only to his fine tact with which he makes specific decisions, but also for the unfortunate formulation which Schäffle has given to the basic principles of his value theory. He remarks quite correctly (p. 175) that consideration of the sacrifices of acquisition and of the utility of goods "have a common root in human sensations." In fact, the phenomena of value must be explained from this common root. But Mr. Schäffle's formula of the "balance" describes suitably neither how nor the extent to which utility and cost participate in valuation.

III
AN OBJECTION AND ITS REFUTATION

We found the source of value in the significance of goods for our well-being. We propose to rank values according to the difference in well-being, that is, the difference between pleasure and pain that depends on the possession or non-possession of an economic good. In final analysis, these are feelings and sensations that must be ranked and taken into account.

Some writers now object that we cannot and must not consider feelings. According to one, they are irrational and incommensurable.[1] According to another, they cannot be ranked. "An object cannot be called 1 ¼ times more beautiful or $1^1/_6$ times more delicate or elegant than another or an individual $1^1/_5$ times more considerate or educated than another. Nor can we say, this picture of my father or the book written by a friend is 1 ¼ times or $1^1/_5$ times more valuable than the picture of my brother or that gift of an acquaintance, etc. All these sensations, wishes, interests, etc. cannot be placed on a denominator and, therefore, cannot be measured."[2]

The inferences drawn from such premises differ widely but all aim at us. Some opponents do admit that subjective value flows from incommensurable personal "interests, wishes, wants, objectives, goals, etc." Therefore, value is deemed to be immeasurable.[3] Other writers readily accept that value can be ranked, even numerically determined, but they deem it impossible for incommensurable human wants, sensations, etc. to determine the degree of value. They believe that measurable value must derive its origin and yardstick from measurable quantities, such as

---

[1] Schellwien, *Die Arbeit und ihr Recht*, Berlin, 1882, p. 198.

[2] Neumann in Schönberg's *Handbuch*, 2nd ed., Part I, p. 159 *et seq.*

[3] Neumann, *ibid.*

labor or production costs.[4] At any rate, both groups agree expressly or tacitly that our science has no use for incommensurable wants and immeasurable subjective values.

If we were to pursue these beliefs to their logical conclusions, they would surpass the expectations of even their authors. If it were true that our wants are completely incommensurable, then all economic action would in fact be impossible. According to the well-known principle of economy, we seek highest utility with smallest cost. But how could we economize, if we are unable to judge which utility is the greatest and which one the smallest, or whether the yield exceeds the necessary sacrifice. How could we judge all this, if it were not possible in some way to compare our wants, wishes, and sensations, to place them on a common denominator and judge their absolute or relative intensities?

In fact, we compare and contrast our subjective sensations and wishes every day and every hour. Even if every want category yields a different kind of enjoyment, this would not prevent us from comparing the degree of enjoyment. It is true, the enjoyment of a cold bath differs greatly from that of listening to symphony, which in turn differs from gratification of a hunger sensation. But everyone knows quite well which one of the three enjoyments is the greatest in a given situation. And while the prick of a needle is quite different from a toothache, we can still conclude that the toothache inflicts greater pain than the prick of a needle. If it were true that our joy and pain sensations were really incommensurable, we would continually suffer greatest confusion. Since the wealth of even the richest man would be insufficient to satisfy all his wants, he would be at a loss about which wishes and wants he wants to satisfy first. And without joking, it could happen some day that, for instance, we could die from thirst in an abundance of water because we could not decide which use was a higher priority, quenching our thirst or watering our fields. The very fact that we do economize is the best proof that our joy and pain sensations are open to intensity determination. The only point of contention can be the means or method of prioritizing our joys and pains.

There is complete agreement on the fact that we are able to

---

[4] Schellwien, *ibid.*

determine that one joy sensation is greater than another. And there cannot be any doubt that we are able to judge whether a certain joy sensation is much greater or merely slightly greater than another. But can we determine the difference even more precisely? Can we determine it numerically? Can we say, for instance, the joy sensation A is three times greater than that of B?

I am convinced that we can. Or, to state it very carefully, we do it sometimes. We must do it for practical reasons because in many cases it is the only way to make reasonable, practical decisions. Again and again we face the situation that we must choose between several enjoyments that cannot be obtained simultaneously because of our limitation of means. The situation may be such that we must choose between one great pleasure and a multiplicity of smaller enjoyments. No one can doubt that we are capable of making such decisions. But it is equally clear that we cannot make such a decision on the basis of a general judgment that the pleasure of one kind is greater than that of another. The same applies to the judgment that the pleasure of one kind is significantly greater than that of another. But our judgment must be specific on how many small pleasures exceed one of another kind. In other words, we must know the ratio of one pleasure to another.

To use a very simple example, let us imagine a small boy who wants to buy fruit with a small coin in his possession. He can buy either one apple or six plums. Of course, he will compare the eating pleasures afforded by both kinds of fruit. To make his decision, it is not enough to know that he prefers apples over plums. He must decide with numerical precision whether the enjoyment of one apple exceeds the enjoyment of six or fewer plums. To approach the situation from a different angle, let us consider two boys one with the apple and the other with the plums. The latter would like to acquire the apple and, therefore, offers his plums in exchange. After deliberating on his eating pleasures, the former rejects four, five, and six plums for his apple. But he begins to waver when seven plums are offered, and finally makes the exchange at a price of eight. Doesn't his trade reveal a numerically determined conclusion that the pleasure of one apple exceeds that of a plum at least seven times but less than eight times?

What the boys do in this example of apples and plums we all do with other serious objects of economic life. Certainly, everyone has faced a situation where he was offered a good that he couldn't afford. But when the price was reduced, let us say, from $30 to $25, he purchased it. He did this because he believed the enjoyment anticipated by the good is greater than $25 but less than $30. Anyone who reflects on his own experience will find numerous examples of similar situations. It is true, countless economic decisions are made habitually without thought. On the other hand, numerous situations require rational economic decisions, calculated decisions on pleasures and pains. In fact, I would like to maintain that in such cases we frequently use a kind of yardstick, to measure the pleasure which we may obtain with money, a dime, dollar bill, ten-dollar bill, hundred-dollar bill, etc. I believe that everyone thinks of the enjoyment which a given amount of money can buy as a specific quantity, thus aiding us in determining whether a certain pleasure is worth the expense. Of course, the enjoyment derived from money differs with every individual; it is smaller for rich people than for poor people. Furthermore, the kinds of pleasure thus weighed differ greatly with different individuals; the pleasures of a man who enjoys fine intellectual pursuits, for instance, differ from those of an uneducated man.[5] But no matter what we may think of the use of sensation intensities as formal units of measure, I believe I have proven that we do not judge only whether a pleasure sensation is greater than another, but that we also try to calculate this difference, on occasion, with numerical precision.[6]

---

[5] A scholar, for instance, who wonders whether he should spend $20 for a certain expenditure may reflect as follows: "For the money I could go to the theatre." A simple farmer whom I knew used to think in such cases: "For the money I could drink 20 glasses of beer."

[6] Someone who likes to split hairs might object to the two statements, "I like an apple as much as eight plums," and "I prefer an apple over a plum eight times" as not being identical. The former statement contains no preference between two enjoyments, but rather expresses that there is no difference between two compared enjoyments. We may be capable of such judgments, but incapable of direct measurements of sensation differences. Readily admitted! But the first statement leads to the second, which is logically included in the first. It may be true that we are unable to determine numerically the difference between the enjoyment of an apple and that of a pear. But if we are able to judge that we like one apple as well as eight plums and one pear as well as six plums, then we must also be able, by way of deduction, to make the third judgment from the first two, that we prefer one apple over a pear by one-third. It is irrelevant for our theory whether we can

(continued...)

I am going to make some concessions. I gladly admit that the term "measurement," at least in its strictest meaning, is not suitable for such analyses; it should be "approximation." It is really impossible mechanically to measure wants precisely the way one measures with rulers and tapes. But it seems to me that we are no worse off than someone who forgot his tape measure and wants to estimate the size of people he meets, or the height of houses and trees he sees. Similarly, I can estimate, without a yardstick, whether a house is high or low, whether it is higher or lower than another house. In fact, I may estimate with some precision whether it is double or triple the size of another house. In the same way, I may determine with some confidence whether the joy of a certain want satisfaction is large or small, whether it is larger or smaller than that of another satisfaction, and, although with lesser precision, how many times it is larger or smaller than the other.

I also admit gladly that such a ranking of wants is not infallible; in fact, it frequently ends unsatisfactorily. For we never feel the pleasure sensations simultaneously, but we base our comparisons merely on recollections or even fantasies that are quite often delusive. Everyone can relate to an instance where a present pleasure is overrated at the expense of a more enduring future benefit. But I must emphasize that the correctness of our theory does not depend on whether this ranking of wants is correct; it depends only on the fact that such a ranking is actually made. Consider the following. We contend that economic value is derived from addition to well-being. Now, it is objected that the height of this addition cannot be precisely calculated because sensations are "immeasurable." We answer and prove that, right or wrong, it is actually calculated relative to other additions to well-being, i.e. ranked. We thereby have proven the truth of the assumption on which we have built. If actual calculations are imprecise or false, they do not refute our theoretical explanation of valuation, they

---

[6] (...continued)
make such numerical determinations directly or indirectly as long as we can make them. The point of view reflected in this note may also be that of Professor Wieser. In his interesting discussions of the "calculability of value" (*Ursprung und Hauptgesetze*, p. 180 *et seq.*) he states that value can be fully measured and calculated, but that we never use different intensities, only equal rankings of intensity.

merely make it imprecise or false. Correct estimation of an addition to well-being leads to correct valuation, imprecise estimation to imprecise valuation, false estimation to false valuation, as can be observed numerous times throughout economic life. Thus, false calculation serves as well to explain false valuation as correct calculation serves to explain correct valuation.

Summing up our assertions and concessions, the following principles seem to emerge irrefutably from our discussion: First, our wants, wishes, and sensations in fact are commensurable relative to other wants, wishes and sensations. The common denominator lies in the intensity of pain and pleasure we feel.

Second, we are able to judge absolutely and relatively the degree of pleasure and pain that depends on a good. And we make this judgment regardless of mistakes.

Third, our estimate of pleasure and pain is the foundation for our valuation of goods. What's more, it is the foundation for our intellectual ranking of significance which these goods have for our well-being and thus for valuation and our practical economic decisions.

Fourth, this leads us to conclude that our science, instead of ignoring subjective sensations, wants, etc. and subjective value based thereon, must search among them for an explanation of all economic phenomena. A value theory that fails to develop the concept of subjective value is built on quicksand. We shall return to this point later.

IV

ECONOMIC VALUE AND THE POSSIBILITY OF MULTIPLE USES

Frequently, an economic good has more than one use. For instance, wood can be used as firewood or lumber, rye for bread, seed or whisky, salt as seasoning or as a supplement in chemical processes.[1] In all such cases the economic good satisfies different wants of varying importance for each use. Furthermore, demand and supply frequently vary from want category to category. And finally, an economic good lends itself to multiple uses, in varying degrees. Because of these factors, the utility which a good may offer in various uses, that is, its marginal utility, also may vary. It is possible, for instance, that a number of boards used as lumber may provide its owner a marginal utility to which we may assign a ranking of 8, while the same boards used as firewood are ranked at 4. In such cases the question arises, which marginal utility determines the value of the good.

The answer is simple: in such cases the highest ranked marginal utility determines the good's value. As described in detail above,[2] the applicable marginal utility is the largest utility to which a good may be applied economically. If there is a choice of several exclusive uses for the good, it is obvious that when acting rationally the most important use takes priority. It alone is economical, all less important uses are excluded from consideration and, therefore, cannot affect the value of the good. In our prior example, if a farmer has covered all his more important needs for

---

[1] Producers' goods often have extraordinary applicability. One and the same piece of iron, for instance, may serve as rail, nail, hammer, anvil, blade, scissors, key, hinge, or in a hundred other forms.

[2] See p. 32.

firewood and lumber with some part of his supply, and two desirable uses with rankings of 8 and 4 are left with only one pile of boards remaining, it is obvious then that he will apply that remaining pile to the more important use and leave unsatisfied the less important want. He will use the boards in construction (utility of 8) and not for fire (utility of 4). A gain or loss of the greater utility of 8 depends on the possession or lack of possession of the boards.

Let us summarize the principle: *In the case of economic goods that permit alternative uses and thereby yield different marginal utilities, it is the highest of the alternative marginal utilities that determines the economic value.*[3] This principle can easily be tested by experience. Most people do not value oak furniture for its "fire value," a good riding horse for "horse meat," a beautiful painting for "old canvas."

We have considered several instances where an economic good has multiple uses. In an advanced market economy nearly all goods can also be employed as media of exchange for other goods. When we use goods for exchange we usually compare one use with all other uses. The terms used to describe "own use" and "medium of exchange" are "use value" and "exchange value."

In a certain sense both kinds of values are subsets of subjective value. Use value is the significance which a good may have for the well-being of an individual provided he uses it directly.[4] On the

---

[3] It may seem that this analysis contradicts our earlier statement. We now deem the *highest* among several alternative marginal utilities the decisive one, while earlier it was the smaller one whenever the direct marginal utility of a good (respectively the utility of the last good of the same category) is greater than its indirect marginal utility (respectively the marginal utility of those goods that are called upon to substitute). (Cf. above, p. 41.). The apparent contradiction is solved easily. In the former case we are concerned with the choice of several uses still covered by the supply, in the latter case with the choice among uses that remain unprovided. As we stated on an earlier occasion (p. 36, note 13.), the smallest still covered use always coincides with the largest of those uses that is left uncovered without the good.

[4] Use value could again be divided into enjoyment value and production value (in a subjective sense) depending on whether own use is for own enjoyment or the production of other goods. Others present a tripartite division into use value, production value, and exchange value. In this case, use value is understood to

(continued...)

other hand, exchange value is the significance which a good has for the well-being of an individual because of its ability to acquire other goods in exchange. The use value, according to our principles, is determined by the marginal utility the good affords in direct use. On the other hand, the subjective exchange value obviously coincides with the use value of the goods that can be acquired in exchange. When I use a good in exchange I gain in well-being precisely what the acquired goods afford in utility. Thus, the magnitude of exchange value is determined by the marginal utility of the goods acquired in exchange. For instance, let us assume that I own a quart of wine which I can exchange for a pound of meat. The use value of the wine is determined by the pleasure of drinking it and its exchange value by the enjoyment of the meat which I may acquire in exchange.

We are saying that the subjective exchange value of a good is identical to the use value of the goods acquired in exchange. It follows that the exchange value depends on two circumstances: first, on the *objective purchasing power* (objective exchange value) of the good; for this purchasing power determines whether we can acquire many or few goods in exchange. And it depends on *the conditions of want and wealth of the owner*, for they determine whether the goods acquired in exchange have a higher or lower use value. For instance, the exchange value of a quart of wine is higher, if two pounds of meat instead of one are obtained in exchange. But in both cases the subjective exchange value will be all the higher the greater the subjective use value of a pound of meat is for its owner. It would be quite erroneous to assume that the subjective exchange value of a quart of wine must be the same for everybody, just because in the market place a quart of wine is exchanged for a pound of meat. The fact is that the pound of meat may be subject to all ranks of subjective use valuation, from the rich living in abundance down to the beggar facing starvation. The same is true for the quart of wine on which the acquisition of the meat depends. For a poor person the quart of wine, with which he can acquire meat that may save his life, has immeasurable welfare significance. For the rich person whose table is well set it may have very little

---

[4] (...continued)
mean merely the employment for direct want satisfaction.

value. Of course, the case of objective exchange value is quite different; it does not concern us here.

It is a common fact that the use value and exchange value of a good may be different for its owner. For a scholar, for example, the use value of his books is usually much greater than their exchange value, while the opposite is true for a book merchant. Again the question arises, which of the two values is controlling in such cases. For a good can have only *one* value for one person. In fact, the value is the significance which a good has for the well-being of an individual. And this significance cannot be simultaneously large and small, high and low.

We are dealing here with the special case for which the general principle has already been elaborated. Employment in own use and in exchange are two different kinds of employment for the same good. If each affords different utilities, then the higher marginal utility is the controlling economic value. If use value and exchange value of a good differ, then the higher one of the two "values" is its primary value. In practical life, we always assign our goods to those employments that yield the higher value. And the use value and exchange value may change with the same individual under changing conditions, which may result in a reassessment of the good's use. While our value literature has explained this point so thoroughly, I merely wanted to mention it and add one further remark.[5]

The separation of value into use and exchange value, which is as old as our science, has recently come under attack. In fact, the distinction has been called untenable.[6] As far as these attacks are aimed at the popular interpretation of this distinction, I deem them fully justified. This interpretation usually assigns a *fundamental difference* that divides all value. But as I endeavored to demonstrate above, there is no uniform value concept.[7] If, nevertheless, the distinction is applied to all phenomena, then quite heterogeneous things that belong to fundamentally different fields can be

---

[5] Cf. especially Menger *ibid.*, p. 213 *et seq.*

[6] Cf. Neumann in *Schönberg*, 2nd ed., p. 156 *et seq.*, especially p. 156, note 70, also p. 163, note 93; then Wolf, *ibid.*

[7] Cf. above, p 6.

categorized in multiple fields. As Mr. Neumann correctly pointed out, use value must then embody not only "subjective value relating to the use by the owner," but also objective nutrition value, heat value, fertilizer value etc. And analogously, "exchange value" would have to embody not only subjective exchange value, but also objective purchasing power which is quite different in content. We need not elaborate on the point that such a distinction is useless and scientifically unfruitful and that it practically prevents a uniform and basic explanation of the phenomena of use value and exchange value.

The same distinction that is untenable as a fundamental difference can be salvaged as one separating only subjective value. In fact, I believe it to be such a significant distinction, whether the welfare significance of a good flows from its direct employment for want satisfaction or from its employment in exchange for other goods, that its emphasis becomes desirable and useful. Therefore, the terms "use value" and "exchange value" are quite suitable. Nevertheless, a further objection remains: the division in use value and exchange value, even in this smaller realm, is not quite complete as it fails to take into consideration gifts, pawning, etc.[8] But this is not important. If someone would like to devise a separate category, he may develop a third concept that includes such uses. If not, there is no objection against mentioning additional important concepts with special terms. At any rate, I deem it better to narrowly define the terms "use value" and "exchange value," which makes them not only harmless but positively useful. This seems wiser than to attempt to purge them completely from scientific terminology. They are too deeply rooted for such an attempt to be successful. If we do not use them properly, they will probably live on as permanent points of contention for our science.

---

[8] Well emphasized also by Neumann, *ibid.*, note 93, a-1.

V
THE VALUE OF COMPLEMENTARY GOODS

It frequently happens that economic utility can only be attained through the cooperation of several economic goods. If one good is missing the complete utility cannot be achieved. Agreeing with Menger, we call these goods that work together to accomplish utility, *complementary goods*. For instance, paper and pen, needle and thread, wagon and horse, bow and arrow, two shoes in a pair, gloves, etc. are complementary goods. This complementary relationship is especially common, yea even without exception, in the case of producers' goods.

Of course, the improvement in well-being offered by complementary goods is also reflected in their valuation. They give rise to a number of situations all of which fall under the general framework of the principle of marginal utility. We must make a distinction between the value that is ascribed to the complete group and that to its parts.

The total value of the complete group usually is determined by the marginal utility which the parts as a group are able to render together. If, for instance, three goods, A, B, and C comprise a complementary group and if the smallest economically permissible utility which a combination of these three goods can afford amounts to 100, then all three together will be worth at least 100.

The only exception to this rule can be found when the value of a good is not determined by the immediate marginal utility of its own category but by that of another category through substitution. In our example, this occurs if each member of the complementary group can be replaced through purchase, production, or substitution from other isolated employment. It occurs if the total loss of "substitution utility" for each member of the group is smaller than the marginal utility they afford as a group. For instance, if the latter is 100, but the "substitution value" of each of the three members of the group only 20, 30, and 40, for a total of 90, then it is the smaller utility of 90 that determines the goods' value not the combined utility of 100 (which replacement units assure at any rate). In such cases, the complementary quality exerts no influence on valuation, which takes place according to the usual principles already discussed. This renders a special analysis superfluous. Therefore, I shall turn my attention to the main case in which the marginal utility achieved through *complementary use* is also the primary value-determining utility.

As we stated above, marginal utility determines the combined value of the group. Depending on the circumstances, considerable differences emerge in the manner in which this total value is distributed among the individual members of the group.

First, if none of the members has more than one use and if none of them can be replaced, then each member has the full combined *value of the group*, while the remaining members are completely worthless. For instance, if I own a pair of gloves worth a dollar, the loss of one glove then constitutes the loss of all the pair's utility and thereby also the whole value, while the remaining glove is worthless. Of course, the loss of either glove produces the same results. Only the circumstances determine which one of the needed gloves constitutes "the whole value" and which one is worthless as a "single" glove. In actual life such cases are relatively rare. But the following case happens more often.

Second, the individual members of the group are capable of rendering services which may be less important than their common complementary employment. In this case, the value of an individual unit does not alternate between "nothing" and "all", but rather between the marginal utility it affords by itself at a minimum, and the combined marginal utility minus the individual marginal utility of the remaining members of a maximum. For instance, if three goods A, B, and C render a combined marginal utility of 100, and if A alone affords a marginal utility of 10, B alone of 20, and C alone of 30, then the valuation of A is as follows: separately A affords a marginal utility of only 10 and, therefore, is worth only 10; but as a member of the group, if we were to sell it, or give it away, A affords a combined utility of 100, and without it goods B and C would render only 20 and 30. Possession or loss of good A thus makes a utility difference of 50. As the final member of the group it is worth 100 minus (20 + 30), as an individual unit only 10.[1] As can be seen, the difference in values does not vary as greatly as in the first case, but it is considerable nevertheless. The following cases occur even more frequently.

Third, individual members of the group are not only employable in other uses but they are also replaceable by other units of its kind. For instance, in the construction of a house, the building lot, bricks, lumber, and labor are complementary. But if a pallet of brick is lost or if some laborers quit, we would not be prevented from achieving the joint utility, i.e. the completion of the house. But we would have to replace the quitting laborers and the lost material. This affects the valuation of complementary goods as follows:

(1) The value of the replaceable units, even if they are needed as "final units," can never exceed their *substitution value*, which considers the loss of utility in uses from which the replacement is drawn.

(2) This considerably reduces the range within which the value of a good may fluctuate either as a final unit or as an individual unit. The marketability of a good, also, greatly reduces this range. The more units there are and the more numerous the employment opportunities, the less important is the difference between the employment from which the needed replacement is drawn (maximum) and the next employment to which a superfluous individual unit could be assigned (minimum value). For instance, let us assume that "goods category A" is comprised not only of good A1, which is used in a complementary group, but also two other goods, A2 and A3. Let us also assume that individually they evidence an importance of 50, 20, 10, etc. Then goods A2 and A3 would cover only uses of an importance of 50 and 20. And if one of these two goods could be used as a substitute for good Al, a

---

[1] The circumstances of the case determine which unit is valued as the "final unit" and which as individual units. For instance, if the owner of a complete group receives a bid for good A, he will value it as final unit and attach a lower value to goods B and C as "individual units." On the other hand, if he receives a bid for good C, he will value it as final unit at 100 minus (10 + 20), which is seventy, and attribute only 10 and 20 to units A and B individually.

utility of 20 would be lost. But if, after dissolution of the complementary group, good Al itself would have to seek individual employment, it would find only the third opportunity with an importance rating of 10. Its value thus would still vary between 10 (individually) and 20 (as "final piece" through substitution). But if there were one thousand units and one thousand employment opportunities, instead of just three, the difference between the 1000th employment opportunity, from which the replacement unit would have to be drawn, and the 1001st employment opportunity in which the 1000th unit would have to find other employment in case of group dissolution, would be very small.

(3) Under such circumstances the value of the replaceable units is determined independently from their specific complementary employment. *The replaceable members are assigned their individual values when calculating the group's combined value. In other words, the replaceable members are attributed their fixed value first. These values are then subtracted from the total value, which is determined by the marginal utility of the combined employment. And the variable remaining value is assigned to the non-replaceable members as their individual value.* If, in our often-used example, members A and B have a fixed substitution value of 10 or 20 respectively, then, if the common marginal utility amounts to 100, we assign an individual value of 70 to the non-replaceable good C. If the marginal utility is 120, we give the non-replaceable good an individual value of 90.[2]

In all the situations described above, the last situation is by far the most numerous in real life. This is why the valuation of complementary goods in most cases follows the last formula, which finds its most important application in the assignment of production yield to the various cooperating factors of production. Nearly every product is the result of the cooperation of a group of complementary goods: land, labor, and capital. The great majority of complementary goods can be replaced at random on the market: labor services, raw materials, fuels, tools, etc. Only a small minority cannot be replaced, or at least not easily. For instance, the

---

[2] If C could also be replaced at a low substitution value, the case discussed above on p. 64 would occur, and the marginal utility of the combined use would be irrelevant for the value of the complementary group.

land under cultivation, the mine, railroad, factory, or even the activity of the entrepreneur with its highly personalized characteristics. As can be seen, our last formula applies to these circumstances. Economic reality confirms this in detail. In real life, we deduct at first the "costs" from total yield. But upon closer examination they do not comprise all the costs, for use of land or entrepreneurial activity also constitute costs. And yet, we merely deduct the cost of *replaceable means of production at given substitution value*, for labor, raw material, depreciation of tools, etc. The rest is credited as "net yield" to the non-replaceable members: the farmer to his soil, the mine owner to his mine, the manufacturer to his factory, the merchant to his entrepreneurial activity. When total yield rises, no one credits the addition to the replaceable members, instead it is credited to the soil or the mine. And in the case of declining yield no one charges lower amounts to "costs." The reduction is charged exclusively to the lower yield of the land, mine, etc. This is done logically and correctly. Only fixed substitution utility depends on goods that can be replaced at any time; the balance of the combined utility depends on the irreplaceable factors.

This concept may also help us to find the solution to a problem that has long plagued our science and which has been declared, perhaps a little prematurely, insoluble. The problem regards the contribution made by each of several cooperating factors to the completion of a product.[3] True, the physical contribution cannot be determined numerically. Thus it remains to be seen whether the value contribution can be determined; at this point we will not embark upon this difficult question.

---

[3] Cf. Bernhardi, *Versuch einer Kritik der Gründe für grosses und kleines Grundeigentum*, Petersburg, 1849, p. 198; Mithoff in Schönberg's *Handbuch*, 2nd ed., p. 692 and the authors mentioned here. Also Wieser, *Ursprung und Hauptgesetze*, p. 170 *et seq.*

VI
THE VALUE OF PRODUCERS' GOODS AND GOODS OF "REMOTER ORDER"

The title of this section suggests that we are embarking upon the discussion of a difficult concept. It is well known that the cost of economic goods exerts an important influence on their value. But it has been a difficult problem for our science to explain both this influence as well as that exerte d by utility. Will we find that cost is a primary source of value, or perhaps even the only one? This is what the socialists teach. But they have so many theoretical contradictions and such obvious inconsistencies between real life and their doctrines that every unbiased theorist rejects them.[1]

If cost is not the only source of value, could it nevertheless be an independent source of value in addition to utility? Several schools of thought teach this, which I would like to call "dualistic." At times, this dualism is merely form because only the subject matter is divided dualistically. Ricardo set the example. In some cases as, for instance, rare goods, monopoly goods, etc., they elevate utility (or scarcity) to be the sole source of value. In other cases, when goods can easily be reproduced the analysts consider cost as the sole source of value. Other writers, like Professor Schäffle, offer an explanation that has comprehensive applicability but suffers from inner dualism. According to them, the value of all

---

[1] I recently subjected the socialist value theory to a comprehensive critique in my *Geschichte und Kritik der Kapitalzinstheorien*, Innsbruck, 1884, p. 427 to 444, (English ed., *History and Critique of Interest Theories*, Libertarian Press, 1959, pp. 241 - 321); I need not return to it at this point.

goods flows from both sources.[2] Both dualistic theories manage to avoid gross disharmonies with the facts. This is easily done, for whoever has a choice of two principles can easily shift from one to the other. But an occasional agreement with the facts can hardly compensate for the inner contradiction.[3] What we need is a theory that explains all value phenomena harmoniously and completely. Here *hic rhodus hic salta* seems to apply to the value theory. (It means "Rhodes is here, here is the place to jump." This is a Latin translation of one of Aesop's fables called *The Braggart* in which an athlete claims that he made a fantastic jump in Rhodes and that he can supply witnesses. The response by one of the members of the audience was, "there is no need for witnesses, you can perform the jump here and now." *Translator*). A difficult jump and comprehensive task for a wholesome value theory is this: neither to deny the "law of costs" nor to explain it ambiguously with a custom-made special principle, but to explain it simply and convincingly with the same general principle that explains the value of all goods including those to which the law of costs does not apply. The following pages are to pursue this task. An analysis of the value of producers' goods shall serve as an introduction.[4]

All goods have in common that they serve the satisfaction of human wants. But only some of them render their services directly; we call them *consumers' goods*. Many others render their services indirectly inasmuch as they are useful in the production of other goods that provide the satisfaction of our wants; we call them *producers' goods*. All producers' goods have in common that their relationship to human well-being is indirect. In turn, they differ again in their degrees of indirectness. For instance, flour from which bread is made is less far removed from final want satisfaction than is the acre on which the grain is grown from which the flour is ground. To clarify our analyses, it is advisable to introduce a goods classification that explains the different degrees of directness and indirectness more clearly than does the common classification of producers' goods and consumers' goods.

---

[2] Cf. p. 48.

[3] See also above, p. 48.

[4] For the whole paragraph cf. the excellent discussions by Menger, Grundsätze, p. 123 *et seq.*, and Wieser, *ibid.*, p. 139 et seq.

Therefore, we would like to classify the goods according to their order of want satisfaction.[5] In the first order are those goods that directly serve our want satisfaction, that is, consumers' goods (for instance, bread). In the second order are those goods which help to produce the goods of first order (for instance, the flour, the bake oven, and the baker's labor that cooperate in the baking of the bread). In the third order are goods that serve the production of goods of the second order (the rye from which the flour is made, the mill that grinds it, the building material of the bake oven, etc.). In the fourth order are the producers' goods for the goods of the third order (the soil that produces the rye, the plow that cultivates it, the labor of the farmer, the building material of the mill, etc.). And so on– in the fifth, sixth, tenth orders always are the economic goods and services that produce goods of the next lower order.

We are searching for the value of producers' goods, or stated synonymously, the goods of "remoter order." One thing is very clear from the outset: their value can neither flow from another source nor can they have different standards from those used to determine the value of other goods. In other words, producers' goods, like al other goods, can only acquire significance for our well-being by enhancing it. The final advantages they afford consist of want satisfaction; their value must be high if an important want satisfaction depends on them, and it must be low if an unimportant want satisfaction depends on them.[6] The only difference is this: with consumers' goods, the economic goods and want satisfaction are directly confronted, while with producers' goods, the goods are separated from their dependent want satisfactions by a long line of intermediary goods, their successive products. This separation of goods from their dependent want satisfaction enlarges the material and scope for new relationships, especially those between the value of producers' goods and that of their products. The primary law of value is neither refuted nor disturbed by this situation. As in the analogous case of "complementary goods," the principle merely needs additional

---

[5] We are following the example of Menger, *Grundsätze*, p. 8 *et seq*.

[6] I believe I need not discuss the instance, which is possible also with producers' goods, where the dependent utility does not consist of want satisfaction but rather of avoiding pain. Cf. above p. 45.

interpretations for the myriad possible applications. It is our task to pursue these interpretations.

Let us imagine a typical production line. A consumers' good, let us call it A, emerges from a group of producers' goods of second order; let us call them G2. They in turn emerge from a group of goods of third order, G3, which in turn are produced by goods of fourth order, G4. To simplify matters let us assume at first that each one of these orders of production is completely used up in the process and that this employment is the only one of which they are capable. Now let us investigate what well-being depends on each group of goods in this production line.

We already know that consumers' good A's marginal utility depends on the last product produced. Therefore, we need to begin our examination with rank G2. Without group G2 we would have to forego product A, that is, we would enjoy one unit less of product category A. But "one unit less" means, as we already know, loss of a want satisfaction, the smallest satisfaction for which one good could be employed economically. In other words, it means the loss of the marginal utility of product A. Product A's marginal utility depends as much on group G2 as it does on the last product A produced. Let us continue with the next rank. Without group G3 we would have to forego the preceding group G2, consequently one unit of consumer category A, that is to say, its marginal utility. Thus, the utility depends on group G3 as it does on the subsequent ranks in the line of production. The same is true with group G4. Without it, we would lack a unit of G3 which otherwise could have been produced. We then would be lacking a unit of G2, a unit A and respectively its marginal utility.

We may now generalize: *one and the same welfare addition, that is, the marginal utility of the end product depends on all preceding groups of means of production*. No one will be surprised about this conclusion. It is obvious right from the outset that a production line that affects our well-being only through its end product neither can acquire nor yield a utility other than that of its end product. The same final utility depends on all preceding ranks of the chain, at times remotely, at other times rather closely.

We may now deduce the following general principles for the value of producers' goods. (1) Because one and the same utility depends on all preceding producers' goods, their value must basically be the same. (2) Their common value, in final analysis, is determined by the marginal utility of their end product. We emphasize *in final analysis*. (3) Moreover, the value of a producers' good receives its *direct* measure from the preceding product of nearest order. After all, the service of a producers' good consists of the manufacture of its products. We appraise it according to the value of the end product for us. In substance, this sentence completely concurs with the former, for the value of goods of nearer order reflects the marginal utility of the end product. All producers' goods derive their value from it; but this derivation proceeds from rank to rank. At first, the marginal utility determines the value of the end product. This value then provides the directive for the value of those goods that give shape to the end product. And this value directs the value of the third group of goods, which in turn directs the value of the last group, the fourth. The name of the decisive factor may change from rank to rank, but it is always the same source that flows through various stages: the marginal utility of the end product.

We can either determine the value of producers' goods by proceeding level by level through to the end product, or we can skip directly to the end product. Skipping directly to the end product's marginal utility gives us a short convenient formula, which in real life is used more often than the main formula. When we estimate the yield of a producers' good for our well-being we naturally look for the product it brings forth and for the addition to our well-being this product supplies. If we don't know this, we must in fact reflect on the whole sequence of utility, rank by rank, until we finally arrive at the marginal utility of the final consumers' good. But this is not necessary most of the time. Past reflections and experiences give us a ready judgment on the value of products. And without further ado we value producers' goods according to this product value. A lumber dealer who wants to buy wood for the manufacture of barrels will not take long to appraise the value of the lumber; he estimates how many barrels he can manufacture with it and knows the present market value of the barrels. He need not bother further.

The thought that the value of a producers' good follows that of its products has suffered a peculiar fate in our literature. It is so self-evident that it seems to have developed on its own. We find it already with Say, later with Hermann, Riedel and Roscher.[7] But these authors probably thought it too self-evident, superfluous to develop or prove, or to incorporate in the system. They merely applied it occasionally when it seemed to fit. But this led to the odd situation that the principle remained, so to speak, an opportunity axiom that was remembered at times, ignored at other times, and therefore failed to enter scientific awareness. It thus remained without influence on general theory. These authors believed in it implicitly but explicitly taught the very opposite. There probably was not one theorist who was not convinced at times that the value of the producers' good "vineyard" depends on the value of its product "wine." Nor was there probably one theorist who did not simultaneously teach the very opposite, that product value depends on cost, that is, on the means of production that are used up in their manufacture. It was left to the sharp and systematic mind of Menger to elevate the old opportunity axiom to the rank of an important scientific principle.[8]

So far we have developed our principles of the value of producers' goods merely from reason, so to speak, as hypotheses of economic logic. Now what is our experience in real life? It confirms the hypotheses. For verification of our theory of marginal utility we may refer to the apparently contradictory "law of costs." Experience shows that the value of most goods equals their "costs," but costs merely are the sum of producers' goods, labor services, capital goods, use of wealth, etc., that are used up in the production of an economic good. The well-known relationship between cost and value is merely another way of saying that the values of successive goods categories of various ranks are equal. However, I am aware that as far as the *cause* of this equality is concerned, the law of costs is subjected to diverse interpretations. We stated that the value of producers' goods is determined by the value of their products. But usually the law of cost is interpreted to mean that the product value is determined by the magnitude of costs, thus by the value of the producers' goods from which they are manufactured.

---

[7] For further details see my *Geschichte und Kritik der Kapitalzinstheorie*, p. 163, 242 *et seq.* , p. 255 *et seq.* Libertarian Press edition, pp. 93, 178 *et seq.*, p. 190 *et seq.*

[8] *Grundsätze*, p. 123 *et seq.*

We will have to analyze this contradiction in detail further below. At this point, I merely would like to emphasize that this value relationship among the successive groups of producers' goods actually exists, no matter what its cause.

It is true, this value equality is not absolute, but merely approximate. We may speak of a *tendency towards value equality*. The deviations from absolute equality are twofold: some are characterized by regularity, others are not. Both are caused by the fact that production takes time. During a long period of time, while the goods of sixth or eighth order gradually move through our intermediary stages into their final form as consumers' goods, men and things may change. Wants may change as well as the relations of demand and supply and man's recognition of them. Goods thus may encounter changes in valuation in their various stages to want satisfaction. Deviations resulting from this source can be very great or small, upward or downward. They are unpredictable.

Moreover, we may observe a constant and regular deviation from complete equality. We may observe that the total value of a complete group of more remote order trails the value of their products at a constant ratio. The magnitude of value difference relates to the duration of time required for the transformation of the producers' goods into their products. For instance, if the value of a product is 100, the total value of labor services, of the use of land and the capital[9] needed in production usually is somewhat less than 100, perhaps 95 if the production process takes one year, perhaps 97 to 98 if the process takes half a year. This value difference is attributable, in part, to interest. Its explanation represents another problem of great interest which I have discussed elsewhere.[10] We

---

[9] Of course, only the depreciation of invested capital can be considered here.

[10] Cf. my work on *Capital and Interest* in connection with my preceding discussion. I merely would like to add the following remarks. The appearance of a small but regular difference that exists between the value of products and their means of production (costs) leads most modern theorists to believe that the clearly visible material costs (labor, use of land, substance of capital) do not represent the total concept of costs, but that there must still be a cost component that constitutes the missing part of the total value. Opinions differ on the nature of this immaterial cost component. Some writers find it in the sacrifice of "abstinence," others in moral "labor" (saving, etc.), others in the "use" or "possession" of capital invested (continued...)

must not confuse it with this analysis. Therefore, I shall ignore this difference in the followup.

In our preceding analysis we developed the law of value of producers' goods under the simplified hypothesis that every group of producers goods permits only a certain single employment. In real life, this hypothesis is applicable only occasionally. In fact, producers' goods evidence a general versatility that is far greater than that of consumers' goods. The great majority is capable of rendering thousands of different services as, for instance, iron, coal, and especially human labor. We must bear this in mind in our theoretical analyses. And we must inquire whether our law (that the value of a group of producers' goods is determined by the value of its products) is subject to modification, and if so, what such a modification should be.

Let us, therefore, vary the assumptions of the typical example. Someone owns a large supply of second order producers' goods (G2). He can use it to manufacture at random either a consumers' good from category A, category B, or category C. Naturally, he wants to cover all his wants and, therefore, will manufacture simultaneously consumers' goods of all three categories according to the demand for each category. For optimal production, the producers' goods will be allocated so that the marginal utility of every unit in each category is approximately equal.[11] Differences, in fact, considerable differences, may occur nevertheless because, as we have already seen,[12] the ranking of specific wants is not always equal and uninterrupted. For instance, the first space heater in a room has considerable utility, let us designate it with the proportional number 200. But a second heater would afford no utility at all. Naturally, I shall cease providing space heaters after the purchase of one unit and its marginal utility of 200, even

---

[10] (...continued)
in production. But many important objections cast doubt on these attempts at explanation. Cf. my *History and Critique*, especially p. 226 *et seq*., (Libertarian Press edition, p. 165), then Chapter VIII on the Use Theories, Chapter IX on Abstinence Theories, Chapter X on Remuneration Theories.

[11] The principle of efficiency requires this. Cf. Wieser, *Ursprung*, p. 148 et seq.

[12] See above p. 29.

though my provisions in other want categories may descend to a marginal utility of merely 100 or 120. Therefore, in order to keep our example true to reality, we must assume that the marginal utility of one unit in each of the three goods categories A, B, and C does vary, let us say, 100 for A, 120 for B, and 200 for C. The question now arises: under such circumstances, what is the value of a G2 group of producers' goods?

We already are experienced in similar situations so that we can answer without hesitation: the value must be 100. For if one of the available groups is lost, the owner naturally shifts his loss to the least sensitive area. He curtails production neither in category B where he foregoes a marginal utility of 120, nor in category C where he foregoes 200. Instead he simply curtails production of category A where he foregoes the well-being of 100. In more general terms, *the value of a producers' good unit is determined by the marginal utility and value of that product which- among all those choices the unit could have produced economically--has the lowest marginal utility*. Thus, all relationships demonstrated above under the simplified hypothesis of single use generally apply also to the relationships between the value of producers' goods and that of their *least important* product.

And what determines the value of the other product categories B and C? This question leads us to the *law of costs*.

If the marginal utility of the category is decisive under all circumstances, then categories B and C[13] must have a value different from that of category A as well as from the value of their costs G2. B must have a value of 120, and C one of 200. But we face one of those cases in which an eventual loss in one category is shifted to another by way of substitution. Therefore, the marginal utility of the latter is decisive also for the former.[14] If a unit of category C is lost, we need not forego the marginal utility of 200 which is afforded directly. Indeed we can manufacture another unit C from a unit of producers' goods G2 and only forego production of a unit of that category in which the marginal utility is the

---

[13] Stated correctly: just one unit of each of these categories; in the text I use the expression for the sake of brevity.

[14] Cf. above, Chapter II, p. 40.

smallest. In our example, this is category A. Therefore, because of the substitution opportunity through production, unit C is not valued for its own marginal utility of 200 but rather for the marginal utility of the least important related product A, which is only 100. The same is true with the value of category B and, in general, with all goods categories that are "production related"[15] with A and whose direct marginal utility is greater than that of category A.

This leads us to several important conclusions. First, the value of goods of higher individual marginal utility is reduced to the level of the value of the "marginal product" and *thereby also to the value of the means of production from which both emerge.*[16] *In short, value and cost are equal here.* This is remarkable because value and cost evolved quite differently from that of cost and marginal product value. The latter was achieved by attributing the value of the means of production to that of the product. In the other case, the product value must adjust to the value of another product, the production-related marginal product. Above all, it must adjust to the value of the means of production from which it emerges and which can be substituted for the marginal product. As the following diagram endeavors to demonstrate, valuation proceeds from the marginal product A to its means of production, or determines its value and then in reverse order ascends from the means of production to the other products B and C that can be manufactured from it.

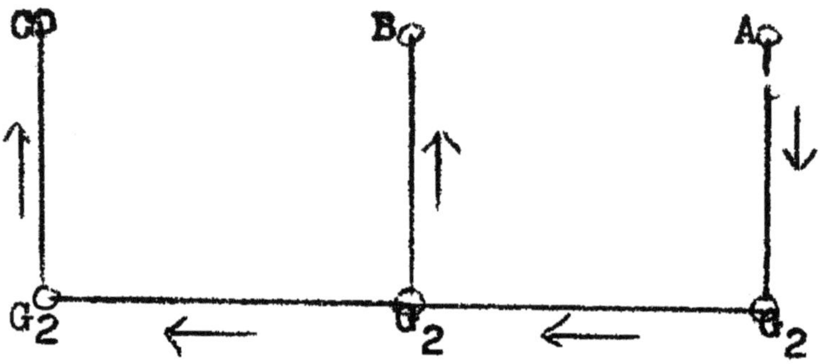

---

[15] Wieser, *ibid.*, p. 146.

[16] For the sake of brevity, this is how we call the product whose marginal utility is the smallest.

The goods of higher direct marginal utility ultimately receive their value from the means of production. To translate this abstract formula into practical terms: reflecting on the value of good B or C, in general, a good of higher direct marginal utility, we must conclude that it is worth as much as the means of production from which the product can be made at any time. If we inquire further into the value of the means of production, we arrive at the marginal utility of the marginal product A. But we usually omit this further investigation because we know the value of the cost items without having to develop them every time from the beginning.[17] In all such cases, we arrive at the value of goods simply by using their costs.

In fact, it is entirely correct to say that costs govern value. But we should always remember the limitations that encompass this "law" and the source from which it flows. *In reality, it is only a law.* It is valid only to the extent that it is possible to quickly acquire substitutable units of production. Without the opportunity to substitute producers' goods the value of every product is determined by the direct marginal utility of its own category, and the connection between the value of the marginal product and the substitutable means of production is broken. This explains why the law of costs is valid only for goods that can be reproduced at will. It further explains why there is only a tendency for costs to govern value. In fact, costs do not precisely determine the value of all related goods, but rather they permit upward or downward deviations when production temporarily trails or exceeds demand.

It is even more important to emphasize that, secondly, even where the law of costs is applicable, *costs are not the final cause of product value.* In final analysis, costs do not give their value to their products but rather receive it from them. This is obvious for means of production that afford a single productive employment. For example, no one would say that tokay wine is valuable because the vineyards are valuable. Instead, they would say that the vineyards are valuable because their products are valuable. The same is true with the mercury mine that receives its value from the mercury, the wheat field from the wheat, the brick kiln from the

---

[17] The division of labor and the exchange economy contribute greatly to the fact that the value of intermediary products is frequently set independently from the value of their means of production.

brick, etc. It is the many-sidedness of the means of production that gives the contrary impression which, upon investigation, proves to be mere appearance. As the moon reflects the light of the sun on the earth, so do many sided means of production reflect the value they receive from their marginal products. The principle of value never rests with the means of production, it rests in the marginal utility of their products.

The law of costs usually is interpreted to mean that costs represent an independent or even the only source of value. This opinion is completely erroneous for many reasons. Above all, it is incorrect to think that the value of the means of production is the cause and that product value is the effect. Product value is explained as being derived from cost, that is, from the value of the means of production from which the product emerged. But whence did the means of production receive their value? Answered consistently: from their costs, thus from the means of production of the third order, which in turn received it from those of the fourth order, and then, from the fifth order, and so on. If we extend this sequence to its origin, we finally arrive at goods that were not produced, for instance, land and human labor. Our explanation thus finds a resting place. But the cost explanation fails even in these cases. Value remains unexplained, unless we resort to another principle. It is conceivable, of course, that these economic goods, are explained by way of a dialectical twist, as products and their value from their costs as, for instance, the value of human labor from the workers means of subsistence. But the explanation never comes to an end. The value of labor is now explained from that of the means of subsistence, bread, meat, etc. Since these are made by labor, their value must again be explained from labor, and so on in a vicious circle.

It therefore should be quite obvious in the case of producers' goods that are capable of single employment only, that their value does not govern the value of the product but instead is governed by it. Such cases not only contradict the law of costs but also cast considerable doubt on those cases in which the law at least apparently has retained its validity. The question then arises, why should the principle of valuation be reversed just because a producers' good is capable of two or several uses instead of just one?

A sensitive theorist cannot help noticing that the advocates of the law of costs, in order to maintain it, must add a number of stipulations that refer to circumstances that have nothing whatsoever to do with cost. For instance, the law is to be valid for goods only that can be reproduced in any quantity, and for these only if they evidence a corresponding degree of utility. For instance, even the advocates of the law of costs readily admit that a ship that does not float is worthless although it may cost a million dollars or would cost a million for its reproduction. All such stipulations are exceptions from the point of view of the principle of cost. If the driving principle of value actually lies in the sacrifices of production, it is hard to see why the principle should fail in this or that case.

The truth is that these stipulations represent conflicting compromises that aim to safeguard the supposed concurrence of the law of costs with reality at the expense of logic. With the help of such stipulations, the cost theory unwittingly stays in touch with the right principle of marginal utility. In fact, *these stipulations alter conditions so that the law of costs concurs with marginal utility theory*. They contain the admission that costs are capable of determining value only if they are supported by marginal utility. Does this not raise the thought that the law of costs is misapplied and that marginal utility theory corresponds better with reality? And does this thought not become clearer when we observe that, in the moment we separate costs from marginal utility, value no longer follows costs but rather marginal utility? In the case of monopoly goods, values rise above costs; and in the case of goods that were produced in excess, value falls below the level of costs. What does this prove? In both cases marginal utility, not costs, determine value. Can we conceive of a more dramatic test of reality?

In my previous discussions I endeavored to elaborate the correct nucleus contained in the law of costs. There is a law of costs; costs actually exert an important influence on goods value. But it is merely a single component within the general law of marginal utility. Whoever believes it to be an independent principle of value commits, in my belief, a crucial error. Other writers have pointed this out many times before me. From Say to contemporary writers many have aimed their critical weapons against the law of costs. If it nevertheless evidences so much tenacity, it is not due to its inner strength, but rather to the circumstance that most opponents merely reject it without replacing it with something better. A dubious explanation was better than none at all. It may be the theory of marginal utility that earns the distinction that it not only tears down but also knows how to build up.

VII

A DEFENSE

Our subjective value theory has been criticized, saying that every man is expected to make unnecessary and complicated deliberations. Calculation of marginal utility is said to require us to line up our concrete wants which a given good may satisfy, then we must line up all the goods in our possession, and finally search for the point of intersection where our gratification can proceed. It entails a cumbersome formula that grows to infinity, especially with goods of remoter order, a calculation that must be made not only for the economic good to be valued but also for all its intermediary products to be valued. Actually our value judgments are not so cumbersome and time-consuming. But why not?

In the first place, continuous practice has made us remarkable experts. Only the beginning reader must spell out every letter of the word. The inexperienced pianist must concentrate on every note in the chord. The same is true of every dilettante in economic life who, when judging the economic situation, must gather every stone of the mosaic to render a value judgment. The experienced entrepreneur does it automatically without much thought. Furthermore, value judgments are much easier for the economic virtuoso to make than for his musical colleague; he usually does not need to be very precise. As long as our valuation errors are not too great we can master economic life's objectives. In fact, excessive deliberation in our value judgments is not only not required by the principle of efficiency but it is forbidden by it. Surely, the most precise value judgments result in the most correct and thus most successful action. Yet the greater precision can only be attained by correspondingly greater sacrifice in time and effort. Up to a certain point the advantage of more careful valuation exceeds the corresponding sacrifice of mental effort. But beyond that point the contrary is true. People who deliberate in detail about every economic decision or value judgment they make regarding every economic good, would have no time for living because of all calculations and reflections. In economic life we follow the correct maxim "Don't be more precise than is worth the effort." In important matters be precise, in average matters be fairly correct, in countless trivialities of everyday life cursory consideration will suffice.[1]

Secondly, in many cases we need not tax our valuation skills in the judgment of economic situations. There are props and aids that greatly facilitate the business of valuation. One such aid is our memory. We need not always completely rebuild our judgment when we decide on economic action. We formed the value judgment earlier, retained it in our memories, and then applied it again later. We may use it as long as our economic situation does not change materially. Economic action for most people takes place in such regular circumstances that old value judgments remain valid for a long time. It would not occur to a housewife who shops daily for her household needs to inquire daily anew into the usefulness and value of a pound of meat, a dozen eggs, a loaf of bread, etc. She merely falls back on her recollections where the respective value judgments are ready-made.[2]

In fact, it is not necessary that such value judgments be derived from our own experience. We receive guidance and instruction and learn to accept the judgment of others who have faced similar economic situations. We follow habits. Before a child can form its own judgment of the marginal utility of various things, he or she

---

[1] In most cases we do not give thought to marginal utility. Does this negate our theory? Certainly not. In every deliberation, even the most cursory, we seek to determine the marginal utility, that which depends on a given good for our well-being. It does not cease to provide the guideposts even in rough estimations. Similarly, who would suggest that we cannot read the mercurial column in a thermometer, if we do not use a magnifying glass to read the degrees in tenths and one hundredths?

[2] Surely, people who suddenly face new circumstances, as for instance, rich people who are reduced to poverty, must form anew their value judgments. They will learn from bitter experience and many an erroneous action that their old attitude towards money, etc. was spurious and is self-defeating in their present situation.

will find impressed upon its memory that a dollar, a chicken, or a pound of steak are valuable goods, and that a penny, or a slice of bread are less valuable, and that a house is much more valuable. In much the same way as a first-grader applies the rules of multiplication and division without having to deduce them himself, and as the student of history retains and relates historic facts without having researched them from the sources himself, we frequently and mechanically base our judgments on what other people have thought out before us.

And finally, the division of labor and exchange assists us when the efforts of valuation would otherwise be most difficult. This is especially true when the value of goods of remoter production order is to be determined. A long line of intermediary products may separate an economic good from its marginal utility; and at every one of the numerous stages of production complementary goods are added to the mix. How difficult it is indeed to retain a clear perception of a good's value over such a complicated chain of production and to maintain with some certainty that "this and no other final utility depends on our good"! Fortunately, this is not necessary. The division of labor has elevated nearly every stage of production to an independent branch of production. Rarely does someone who possesses a good of remoter order take it through all phases of production to its final form as a consumers' good just to enjoy its dependent marginal utility. He merely adds value to it and then sells it to an entrepreneur of the next production stage. This is why he need not be concerned about the subjective value the good may have for him and about its later stages that lie beyond his sphere of interest. He merely raises the question: how many goods of the next higher order can be made and what will be their value, that is, their exchange value? These are very simple questions which everyone can easily answer within his area of expertise.

The intellectual effort which our subjective value judgment thus entails is not as impressive as it first appears. On the other hand, even if the effort were greater than it actually is, we could trust people to undergo this effort. Wherever individual advantage is concerned, where every error is felt as a loss, even the common man becomes sagacious and careful. Indeed, people have given excellent testimony to their caring in economic matters because they recognized the nature of value much earlier than did economic science. Misled by a confusion of utility and value, science elevated air and water to the highest use value. The common man observed and felt correctly; he treated them as things without value. And for thousands of years before our science developed the theory of marginal utility common man was accustomed to striving for goods or foregoing them. He was not in pursuit of the highest utility of which they were capable, but instead he was mindful of the gain or loss of specific utility that depends on every good. In other words, he practiced the doctrine of marginal utility long before theory discovered it.

VIII

THE SCIENTIFIC SIGNIFICANCE OF SUBJECTIVE VALUE

We now know how every individual ascribes value to economic goods that affect his interests. But the question has been raised: how do these highly individual value judgments concern economic science? Isn't the object of this science market economic phenomena rather than individual economic phenomena? We do not want to know the judgment that is rendered in the soul of an individual but rather that which is rendered and ratified by the "meeting of individuals on mutual want," i.e., economic society. In short, we expect to explain and determine not the subjective but the *objective market value*.[1]

Subjective value, nevertheless, is extremely important for our science. In fact, it is so important that hardly enough consideration is given to it. I shall endeavor to demonstrate briefly why this is so.

---

[1] Many theorists probably hold these views. H. Dietzel has given them especially sharp and eloquent formulation in the *Yearbooks*. In a review of Wieser's work, which deals exclusively with subjective value, Dietzel casts Wieser's work out of economics into psychology. (*Jahrbücher*, Vol. XI, Part 2, p. 161 *et seq.*). According to Dietzel, it is the task of the value theory "to search for the hidden source that determines the irregular waves of price, their rises and falls, the secret power which, in spite of the subjective views of men and in spite of the ever changing nature of man, permits the formulation of certain laws of exchange value of material goods with objective certainty." He doubts that "we can use, as our point of departure, subjective value sensations with any promise of success for the elucidation of the complicated phenomena of social economic life." He is missing the bridge "that leads us from the subjective use sensation of the individual to the bustle of economic society. "In many points I agree with this esteemed scholar, but I regret greatly to disagree with him on such a fundamental question. I would be very happy, if my present discussions would lead to a new exchange on these problems about which the last word has not yet been spoken.

"Social laws," which economic science is to analyze, rest on congruous actions of men. This congruity again is the result of congruous motives that guide human action. It can hardly be doubted that an explanation of social laws has to reach back to the propelling motives that guide individual action; it has to make them the starting point. And the more we know of the propelling motives and their relationship to economic actions of man, the more we know of the working of the social laws.

The most powerful motive is our consideration of our well-being. It is, in fact, the only motive whose effect is so all-pervasive that it brings forth distinct laws in spite of any contrary influences. Our consideration of well-being may concern our own person or other individuals in our occasional or permanent economic care. Subjective goods' value arises when we view economic goods from this point of view. Goods' value automatically reflects the existence and strength of this most powerful motive. Wherever we find economic value our well-being is engaged and economic motivation is at work. Furthermore, the magnitude of value reveals the strength of this motivation. Subjective value thus becomes both compass and the universal intermediary motive of human action. It is the compass, for it points out the direction of well-being concern and subsequent action. It is the intermediary motive, for we realize that value is the true mirror of our welfare interests and, therefore, is used in our economic lives to pursue the greatest value.

The next question is whether our science, which is to investigate and explain the principles of man's economic actions, should not carefully analyze the nature of those phenomena that offer the key to an explanation of economic well-being. No one can deny that in consumption, production, and exchange, we adjust our behavior towards economic goods according to the value they afford us. We always aim to gain as much value as possible and to lose as little as possible. Furthermore, it is clear that it is the steadfastness of this motive that gives rise to a regularity in our economic actions.[2] Can we be expected to ignore such an insight

---

[2] J. Neumann describes very well the theoretical significance of value. In his own words: "It undoubtedly belongs to the most important of all economic (continued...)

into the nature of this all-important subjective value, in the conditions of its existence and the determination of its magnitude? It is hardly conceivable that this could and should have been asked of us!

Let us investigate the reasons.[3]

My opponents do not doubt "that, in final analysis, the laws of human wants guide the social forces of production and consumption and, thereby, the mutual exchange values of material goods." But it is not the task of economics, we are told, to explain how our interest in economic wealth and how subjective value sensations can emerge from this most basic motivation of human action. It is not its task "to trace the reasons and principles of human interest in the world of material things." Economics should accept certain motivating force, this "interest in wealth," as ultimately given. The task of economics should begin with a demonstration of how the social phenomena of objective exchange value emerge under given conditions of economic interest and corresponding subjective value sensations.

It seems to me that this train of thought neglects to make a fine but important distinction. We agree that it is not the task of economic science to explain the general principles of human wants, for instance, the existence and effect of our desire for well-being. It can and must leave this to psychology. But it is quite a different matter to show how this desire for well-being affects economic goods and how basic motivation turns into concrete economic interest. Such explanations cannot be expected of general psychology; but whenever they are needed, we call on no other science but economics.

Let us illustrate the point with a concrete example. We all have

---

[2] (...continued)
concepts. It basically determines income, yield, wealth, well-being, riches, etc. It also provides the impetus for production, exchange, purchase, yea, nearly all transactions. And it is an important factor in the formation of price and thus of wage, interest, and rent. *Yes, it can be said, it is the true center and cornerstone upon which hinges and moves all the bustle of our economy*." (Schönberg's *Handbuch*, 2nd ed. Chapter l, p. 165).

[3] I am referring again to the recent discussions by H. Dietzel, *ibid.*, which, in spite of their brevity, present the principal difference with clarity and sagacity.

the strong desire to protect our lives, especially to guard against hunger and thirst. Psychology may explain the source of this desire and why, for instance, it is so much greater than that for musical entertainment. Economic science must accept the existence of this desire and its given intensity. But it is a quite different question why a given desire affects certain economic goods and makes them important for us while, at other times, it fails to do so. Without change in its intensity, why is it at times of highest and at other times of lowest importance? We always have the desire to protect ourselves from hunger and thirst, and food and drink serve to satisfy them. Why is it then that, in spite of the great intensity of this motive power, we cling only occasionally to water and bread, and why we usually show little interest in their possession, or even none at all? The answer to this question cannot be left to general psychology for which it would be superfluous. But an economist must be at home in this instance, if he is to understand the behavior of man towards goods and subsequently to explore the social principles of exchange value.

Those theorists who neglected the theory of subjective value usually believed that the matter was too simple and self-evident to require a special theory. They believed that man desires an economic good all the more the more urgently he needs it; and no special theory was needed on whether or not the good was urgently needed. In my belief, the matter is not so simple and self-evident. The fact that the older theory, which lacked the subjective value analysis, went astray supports my belief. It mistook value and usefulness and consequently ascribed highest value to goods that do not involve human well-being and very little value to those goods that greatly affect it. It even mistook the reason for man's concern for economic goods and rested value on expenditure of labor or other costs. This was not surprising. No matter how simple the theory of marginal utility, of complementary goods, and of the value of goods of remoter order may be, once discovered, it was not so easy to develop from the complex phenomena of economic life. Whoever sought to find his way through the labyrinth of human material interests without its help was bound to go astray.

In this situation Professor Dietzel appeals in vain to the example of British-German literature which never dealt with the value theory as a theory of subjective value. The example would be more effective, if British-German thought had been successful in explaining objective value in spite of its neglect of subjective value. However, I believe that it failed. And had it been otherwise, our literature would not resound with complaints about the incomplete, immature state of our science.

Let us quickly survey its achievements. Three price laws are in vogue in our literature. One ascribes the height of prices or their "exchange value" to the relationship of *demand and supply*, another to *costs of production*, and the third more specifically to the quantity of *labor* used in production or reproduction. This last "law" has been refuted so repeatedly and successfully[4] that it has few followers outside the socialist parties, which are guided by other than theoretical reasons. Next, the law of cost is only a *particular* law of price that is inapplicable to many important goods.[5] Furthermore, it is not an independent law as it borrows its validity from the law of demand and supply. In fact, prices tend to seek the level of costs only inasmuch as demand and supply guide them continuously in that direction. The law of costs thus leads to the law of demand and supply, which constitutes the mainstay of our price knowledge.

What then is the usefulness of this knowledge? It is undeniable that the law of demand and supply is an old and able principle in the inventory of our science. But it is far from perfect even though it has come a long way in the able hands of such writers as Hermann and Mill. It has been around from the beginning of our science and has failed to satisfy ever since. The search for improvement and extension continues. But so far the law of demand and supply has not led us to our goal. This sentiment was emphatically stated by an eminent representative of the price theory who called the formula of demand and supply "empty and meaningless" and its usefulness that of a good "slogan."[6]

Without a good theory of subjective value our investigations into objective value must remain unsatisfactory. At any rate, they

---

[4] Cf. especially Kniess, *Der Kredit*, 2nd Part, Berlin 1879, p. 60 *et seq*. Cf. also my *History and Critique of Interest Theories*, p. 333 *et seq*.

[5] For instance, for all land, all monopoly goods, and other rare goods.

[6] J. Neumann in Schönberg's *Handbuch*, Part II, Essay I, p. 289.

do not render our search for better answers superfluous or hopeless. Surely, the matter is worth an examination, which we endeavor to conduct in the following second part of this essay. Although I do not cherish appeals to authorities where theories speak for themselves, I cannot resist one remark. Until recently the subjective value, or the "use value" as it was commonly called, received scanty attention only from the nation of "ponderers," in German literature. By now the most original thinkers of other nations, such as Jevons, Pearson, and Walras, have begun simultaneously, each in his own way, to use the new theory of marginal utility in the development of the principles of exchange value. Does this not give strong support to the fact that the subjective value theory is more than idle mental gymnastics but rather a fertile foundation of our science?

PART II

THE THEORY OF OBJECTIVE EXCHANGE VALUE

I
INTRODUCTION

Whenever we use the word "value" and, especially, "exchange value," we do not always think of the effect a good may have on the economic well-being of an individual. When we state that a pound of gold, for instance, has a higher exchange value than a pound of iron, we think neither of a particular individual nor of the effect the possession of the good may have on his or her want satisfaction. But we have in mind merely the purely objective fact that we may exchange more goods for a pound of gold than for a pound of iron. This means, there is an objective value concept that differs fundamentally from the subjective concept, as we already demonstrated in Part I of this essay. Value, in the *subjective* sense, is the significance a good possesses for the well-being of an individual; *subjective exchange value* is the welfare significance a good acquires for an individual through its capacity of exchange. Similarly, exchange value, in its objective sense, merely is the capacity of a good to procure other goods in exchange. *Objective exchange value is exchange power.*[1]

In contrast to the subjective value that rests on individual judgment, the objective exchange value is also often called *social economic value*. I cannot recommend this terminology. Of course,

---

[1] Adam Smith already calls exchange value the "power of purchase." (Book I, Chapter IV). Other proposals seem to be less suitable, such as "ratio of exchange" by Jevons (*Principles* 2nd ed., p. 88) or "exchange base" (Ruilvoet, Pierson, *Leerboek der Staathuishoudkunde* 1884, Part I, p. 48). These terms have a connotation that makes it impossible to use them as adjectives or to speak of a greater or lower height. This is why they constitute no satisfactory replacement for the term "exchange value" in countless phrases in popular as well as scientific language. They would require cumbersome definitions while the term "exchange power" can be easily replaced in substance and language.

no objection could be raised, if it merely were to emphasize that this value makes its appearance only in society and through society, in short, that it is the social economic value phenomenon *per eminentiam*. But this interpretation usually is mingled with the thought that exchange value is the very value of an economic good for the national economy. It is interpreted to reflect the judgment of society that ranks above those of individuals, giving significance to a good for all people. It is, so to speak, a value judgment by an objective, higher authority. This is misleading. It is true, as we shall see later, objective exchange value is the resultant of the subjective value judgments of many individuals. But it is not permissible to interpret the determination of exchange value as a *common* judgment, and especially not as a value judgment rendered in the name of and from the point of view of society.

The concept of exchange value is closely related to that of price; but it does not coincide with it. Exchange value is the *ability* to acquire a quantity of other goods in exchange; price is this very *quantity of goods*.

This seems to be the most simple and healthy solution to an argument that has occupied our science for much too long. The older interpretation, according to which price was the exchange value of goods expressed in money, is completely untenable and has been abandoned in recent times.[2] In fact, Professor Neumann correctly remarked that "both, price and value, are usually expressed in money, and both could also be stated in rye, or wheat, or any other marketable commodity."[3] But Professor Neumann himself defines the difference between the two concepts as follows: "Price usually rests on one-sided or two-sided *determination* while value emerges preferably from *estimates* or appraisals." He then designates "in particular" no fewer than three different concepts within this general explanation: First, the circumstance, second, the price at which one item has been exchanged or can be exchanged for other items after one-sided or two-sided determination, and third, the *good itself* that has been or can be exchanged for another

---

[2] For instance Malthus, *Definitions in Political Economy*, No. 47: Price equals the quantity of money for which a commodity exchanges, etc.

[3] Schönberg's *Handbuch*, 2nd ed., Part I, p. 174.

thing after one-sided or two sided determination.[4] In my belief, only the third of these interpretations is acceptable. The first two are unfortunate and superfluous concessions to popular language; popular language does not require them. In fact, in the very phrases which Professor Neumann cites as proof that concepts one and two are needed, the term "price" may be replaced with "goods quantity" or "exchange good" in the third sense.[5] If, nevertheless, in some metaphoric or elliptic phrases the term price should be used in such a way that it deviates from its basic meaning of "exchange good," it is not the concern of scientific terminology to support or sanction such deviations. Where would we get if we were to formulate a scientific concept for every imprecise or figurative phrase of popular language! We need discipline for our terminology; we must not tolerate double- or triple-meanings unless cogent reason requires it. There is no such reason in this case. Therefore, we are reluctant to give our scientific price concept any meaning other than that of *exchange good* which a good acquires or can acquire in exchange.

We do not obtain a proper picture of a good's power of exchanges by just looking at the quantity of one other category which the good may obtain in exchange. In fact, a certain height of price can be caused not only by low purchasing power of the first good but also a high exchange power of the second good. To ascertain the exchange power of an economic good, we must analyze either its exchanges toward numerous other goods or toward a good that is commonly used as a yardstick. Such a good is money. We simply measure the exchange power of goods by

---

[4] *Ibid.*

[5] For the meaning of the first, Neumann cites a section from the Code of Commercial Law according to which in case of certain damages the compensatory value is determined by the market price and "in absence of a market price" by the findings of experts. These words must be interpreted to mean that value is determined by the goods quantity regularly available in exchange for the respective goods and, if this quantity cannot be ascertained, by experts. In the same manner, we may substitute "exchange good" for price in the sentence "water, ice, and snow obtain a price at such times." And for the meaning of the second, he cites that "the price of land in our city has fallen or risen recently." Also here we may say: "the goods quantity that can be exchanges for land in this city has risen," which is better than "the degree in which we may exchange other things for land has risen or fallen!"

their money prices.[6]

---

[6] Naturally, necessary consideration must be given to the changes in the yardstick itself,to the value of money.

II
THE PROBLEM

For ages it has been the most important task of the value theory, indeed, one of the most important tasks of economics, to find the law that explains the purchasing or exchange power of economic goods.

Even though the concept of exchange power does not coincide with that of price, their principles do coincide. Not only does the law of price explain why a good *actually attains* a certain price, but it also offers information on *why* it is *capable* of attaining this price. The law of price comprises the law of exchange value.[1]

We are speaking of a law of price. Can there really be such a law?

A few decades ago this question would have been superfluous.

With naive confidence the older price theory did not doubt for a moment that there was a regularity in goods prices, nor that it was its duty to discover this regularity and formulate it in "price laws." The fruits of its indefatigable search were expressed as the "law of demand and supply" and "the law of costs." The situation is quite different today. Methodological doubts arose that questioned not only the popular faith in the traditional laws of price but also the laws themselves. Skepticism gradually crept from methodological writings, where it first appeared, to theoretical economics. This skepticism decidedly influenced two German theoretical treatises on price theory.

Professor Neumann represents moderate skepticism. He

---

[1] Neumann expresses the same thought rather awkwardly in a section dealing with the laws of price. He uses the term "price" as a synonym for "exchange or purchasing power." (Schönberg's *Handbuch*, Vol. II, Chapter I, p. 263 *et seq.*)

defends "so-called" economic laws with some sympathy.[2] They are said to be important especially in the field of price theory; without them, he doubts there would be a scientific price theory.[3] At the same time, he piles reservation upon reservation, rejects entirely the law of demand and supply, and then contrasts his relatively short presentation of the tendencies of *regularity* with a long discussion showing how he believes prices actually are formed.[4]

The new treatise by Cohn reflects an even greater break.[5] While the older price theories were preoccupied with analysis and presentation of price laws, Professor Cohn has no use for such laws. The old school concentrated its strength on formulating economic laws as clearly and precisely as possible, but Professor Cohn diligently avoids any formulation that could resemble a "law." It is true, the reader learns many facts, influences, and causes from which the old school discovered the law of demand and supply and the influence of production costs; however, Professor Cohn also deprives them of their origin, evolution, and of their "pretentious form." A reader who studies Cohn's price theory thus can stay utterly ignorant of those laws to which many generations of scientists devoted their greatest efforts to develop.

Has this not gone too far? Professor Cohn himself described in glowing colors the demands which life makes on science;[6] but is life not short-changed, if we deprive it of "laws" simply because they do not yet offer all the answers? If suddenly all economic writers were to imitate the example of Cohn, the coming generation would learn nothing of these laws. While we may eliminate some errors, don't we also lose an important part of our knowledge of life?

To answer this question in detail, I would have to raise the great methodological question of the very existence of inexorable economic laws. But this is neither the time nor the place. Furthermore, more qualified authorities recently analyzed the

---

[2] Schönberg's *Handbuch*, Vol II, Chapter 1, p. 148 *et seq.*

[3] *Ibid.*, p. 268.

[4] *Ibid.* , pp. 296 - 334.

[5] *Grundlegung der Nationalokönomie*, Stuttgart 1885, p. 487 *et seq.*

[6] Preface

problems with clarity and objectivity, so that general agreement seems assured. And I basically agree with them.[7] Therefore, instead of launching a general methodological discussion, I merely would like to develop my positive beliefs on what has to be done in the field of price theory. An analogy may simplify my presentation.

If we throw a stone into the middle of a tranquil pond, we see the circles of waves spread in all directions with perfect purity and regularity. But on high seas, winds do not always blow in the same direction and with equal strength, which generates a wave movement that by and large reveals a regular pattern; but when examined in detail, it also reveals many small deviations and irregularities. If the wind should suddenly change or the waves beat upon a coastline with irregular cliffs, there develops a wild pell-mell of crosscurrents, known as surf, whose only law appears to be lawlessness itself. The cause of the difference is easily found. In the first case, a single causation manifests its peculiar regular effects undisturbed by any interruption. In the second case, different forces exert their influence, although one of them is preponderant and capable of exerting a greater influence. In the third case, finally, a wild mixture of counteracting forces leads to an equally wild mixture of motions that act upon each other, erasing any semblance of regularity to the casual observer.

In my belief, analogous causes also have analogous effects in the field of price phenomena.

Human action in general and human behavior with regard to exchange are guided by motivation. We may enumerate two such motives (selfishness and altruism) from among hundreds of possibilities. (For instance, the striving for direct economic gain; the desire for indirect advantage through attraction of customers, elimination of competitors; aversion to purchase from a personal

---

[7] I am referring to Adolf Wagner's methodological discussions in his essay on "Systematic Economics" in Volume XII of the *Yearbooks*, especially pp. 229-242. Also compare Menger's revolutionary "Investigation into the Method of Economics," who differs little from Wagner in the crucial questions, and H. Dietzel's excellent "Contributions to the Method of Economics," *Yearbook*, Vol IX, pp. 17-44 and 197-259. Cf. also E. Sax's pertinent writings *On the Nature and Tasks of Economics*, and E. von Philippovich on *The Objective and Method of Economics.*

enemy or political or national opponent; antisemitism, vanity, anger, stubbornness, revenge; desire to afford an economic advantage to someone because of generosity of affection; desire to punish him, improve him, etc.) Whoever undertakes to explain the motives of men in the determination of prices cannot avoid a detailed enumeration of motives, no matter how many may be combined together in general categories. Small variations in motivation frequently lead to opposite effects in human action. For instance, the desire for our own economic advantage will have quite different effects depending on whether our advantage is the direct objective or merely an indirect one, as, for instance, through underselling of an undesirable competitor. In the first case, keen selfishness leads us to sell our commodities at a high price, in the second case at a low price. The basic motive, vanity, may lead to opposite effects, depending on whether our vanity seeks to appear larger than life or to be economical and a good buyer.

In a given situation, every motive tends to guide human action in a certain direction. If we were always motivated to earn the greatest possible exchange gain, all the characteristic effects of such motivation could manifest themselves clearly in our actions. And prices emerging under our exclusive influence would scarcely be less regular than the even waves set into motion by the stone thrown into the pond. In fact, this is how our science built the "law" of demand and supply i.e. on the sole basis of self-interest. And this law professes to announce, with the certainty of a mathematical formula, the height of prices that results from a given state of demand and supply.

Reality is quite different. We usually act under the influence of several or many counteracting motives which in turn vary in number, kind, and intensity. Naturally, also their effects intersect which influences but does not completely destroy the regularity in our actions. If the regularity of our actions were destroyed, the thought of a "law of demand and supply" would never have sprung up; however, our multiple motives have caused "problems" for the law. Price follows the formula precisely only in some cases. In other cases, an occasional tendency towards regularity may emerge, but with frequent exceptions. And finally, price may run completely counter to the "law of price" as, for instance, in cases of generosity cloaked as a sale.

This is the material for the price theorist. Its nature raises two questions that must be answered right away. *Are those instances that merely approximate the "law of demand and supply" or even disregard it entirely without any rule or law? How can our theory explain these apparent exceptions?*

Our analogy points the way toward the answer to both questions. For a layman, the confusion of the surf may appear "lawless." But a physicist would only smile about the notion that there can be waves without the rules of strict regularity. In fact, he would explain that the most complicated surf is simply the result of clashing currents or waves. He would say that the impact of a wave on a certain beach, colliding with returning waves or other waves that approach from various angles, can, according to the general law of wave motion, generate only very complex notions. But to the layman it appears to be quite lawless.

Brief reflection will allow us to view apparently lawless price phenomena in similar fashion. If the regularity of human action is caused by equal motives leading to equal action, then we must also realize that unequal motives lead to unequal actions. If we know, for example, that a seller has as a secondary objective the granting of a gift to the buyer, we can readily see why the sales price is below the market price. Similarly, we would not be surprised to learn that the wave hitting a beach acts differently from the wave that unfolds in the open sea, or about the feather that falls differently in a vacuum from the one falling in air, or about a double charge that gives a bullet a greater velocity than one with only a single charge. Similarly, in the world of human action a difference in effect flowing from different causes is no exception but instead the result of the interaction of different causes.

How shall our science discharge its obligations in those cases that appear to be "lawless" but are merely complicated by the many interacting actions?

Once again let us borrow an example from the physicist. He first develops the *law of basic phenomenon, that is, the wave motion that develops under the condition of a single simple cause.* When this is found he proceeds to investigate the effect of additional influences individually. He investigates a wave hitting an obstacle, for instance, a solid wall. He analyzes the case of a right angle impact and then a small angle impact. He further develops the laws of "interference phenomena" that analyze a collision of several waves. He does so for various typical cases: some waves may run parallel, others may intersect; some may move in the same direction, others in opposite direction; wave lengths may be equal or unequal; wave peaks and valleys may coincide or differ by half a wavelength or any other size, etc. Of course, our physicist will not investigate every single causation; but he may classify various types depending on the nature of research. For instance, he may be satisfied with developing the law of "wave impact" on a solid wall but ignore the irregularities of the wall. If, for example, it appears that a certain wall shape becomes important, the physicist will include its shape in his scope of the investigation.

After our physicist has individually investigated all the causes of wave motion, he searches for evidence of a coincidence of many or all causes. He dissects the surf, which at first sight appears so chaotic, into a multiplicity of single motions each of which follows its own law and well-known regularity. He would deem it both absurd and futile, if someone wanted to explain the "interference phenomena" without first elaborating the law of simple wave movement.

I believe that the price theorist has good reason to proceed in similar fashion. He, too, must begin by developing the law of the simple *basic phenomenon.* Should he fail to clarify how the determination of price proceeds under the influence of a single motive, he will struggle in vain for an understanding of complicated phenomena that result from an interaction of many competing motives. But what is the basic phenomenon?

Seen purely psychologically, each one of a hundred individual motives that may influence an exchange is competing with others. For instance, the desire for our own gain may equal our desire to make a gift to someone. Therefore, from a purely psychological point of view, an insoluble conflict may arise: which of the hundred possible motives is to serve as "basic cause" and its effects as "basic phenomena"? The choice of motive to follow may be impossible to make without the help of additional information from outside sources.

There is a considerable difference in scope and force with which single motives exert their influence on exchange. One motive emerges above all others: the *desire for direct exchange gain*, i.e. to profit from an exchange of goods. Quite natural! Exchange is a process by which we aim to acquire something against payment. It lies in the nature of things and is proven by experience that this desire for exchange gain is never completely absent (except for wash sales); in most cases it constitutes the primary motivation for our exchange transaction. This leads us to regard the price phenomena that result from our desire for exchange gain as the "basic phenomenon," its law as the "basic law," and the variations that flow from the competition of other motives as mere modifications of the basic law. We act like the physicist who analyses the behavior of falling bodies. In his investigations he considers the force of gravity as "basic force," the fall of a body under the exclusive influence of gravity, that is, in a vacuum, as the basic phenomenon, and the influence of resisting media, such as air, water, etc. merely as resistance, restraints, etc.

The task of the price theory, therefore, seems to be divided into two parts. The first part must develop the *law of basic phenomenon in its purest form*, that is, a law without exceptions, a law that can be applied with consistent regularity. Price phenomena are then analyzed while assuming that the only motive of all exchange participants is the desire for direct gain.[8] It is the task of the second part *to incorporate the modifications that result from additional motives and influences.* Here is the place to elaborate, either in rough estimation or in all detail, the influence which common motives such as habit, custom, fairness, humanity, generosity, convenience, pride, national and race hatred, etc. exert on price determination. It is also the place where we must elaborate upon the effects which institutions, such as monopolies, cartels, coalitions, boycotts, government price regulations, civil and criminal courts,

---

[8] The assumption must be narrow to assure the purity of the basic phenomenon. We often take merely the "desire of economic gain" as general motive, or even more generally "self-interest." Special motives then may guide our actions in the very opposite direction, as we mentioned above (p. 483). Also Neumann, *ibid.*, p. 286. He goes too far, however, when he calls for the assumption that self-interest must be of a certain intensity and strength. If there is only self-interest in our hearts, even its weakest manifestation will guide our actions in the same direction as the strongest manifestation. Only if self-interest prevails over competing motives will the intensity of our motives influence the direction of our actions.

labor unions, and many other organizations exert on the formation of price, just like artificial "wave-breaking."

The attention which each of the two parts of the price theory has enjoyed throughout the years has changed with the fashions of methodology. As long as the abstract deductive method of the English school was in fashion, only the first part was discussed. Later, when the German historical method dominated, emphasis was given to the exceptions as well as to the general rule. Consideration was also given to the influence of national, social, and individual peculiarities. Unfortunately, this new attention did not adequately compensate for the earlier neglect of the second part. Instead, the second part was given exclusive attention with less laudable results and understandably excessive zeal.

This is where prevailing doctrine still seems to be today. I cite J. Neumann as my primary witness. I already mentioned above that he is no extremist, and that his discussions are of special interest to us. With fine methodological tact he made the twofold division of the price theory we recommended, but he did so using inaccurate terminology. He first dealt with general regularities of prices and then, in a separate section, with "actual price determination."[9] But in content as well as emphasis of its systematic importance he greatly neglected the first general part. In fact, he argued more against than about the general law.[10] It is rather clear how much he labors under the influence of prevailing one-sided fashion.

In the following pages I propose to deal exclusively with the first part of the price theory. I hope to develop clearly the basic law of price presuming the exclusive rule of the desire for direct exchange gain. To prevent any misunderstanding right from the outset, I would like to emphasize that I am not at all pretending to offer the whole explanation of price phenomena. Furthermore, I realize that the preceding discussion requires completion of the second part as well. Nevertheless, I can easily justify why I limit myself to the treatment of the first part. In the first place,

---

[9] Schönberg's *Handbuch*, 2nd ed. p. 286 *et seq.,* sections 2-4, then 5.

[10] Cf. especially Neumann's drastic discussions on p. 296, which reveal a very low opinion of the general "law of costs." He rejects entirely the "law of demand and supply."

elaboration of the second part would require much more space than is allotted to me at this point. It seems to me that the first part requires special attention today while the second part is treated carefully and successfully by the prevailing doctrine. And finally, I cannot and will not deny that I deem the general part incomparably more important, no matter how well I recognize the scientific importance of the second part. I cannot imagine a satisfactory price theory, if it does not rest on a basic law of price that can be applied with consistent regularity. I am prepared to meet with considerable resistance to my price theory. However, to overcome the resistance with formal proof seems to be neither suitable nor possible considering the subjective nature of the argument.

I merely would like to remind my opponents of one point that offers important proof for the methodological significance of a basic price law built on the hypothesis of self-interest. Even if, in actual life, the so-called basic motive is swayed by hundreds of other motives, by humanity, custom, and the influence of institutional laws, the actual determination of price is not greatly deflected from the direction in which the exclusive impact of self-interest would direct it. I gladly admit that small differences in utility and scarcity or in production costs are overshadowed by one's motives and influences from society, etc., thus reducing their effects. But great differences always emerge victoriously. Can it be denied that in general the market price for a large estate is higher than that of a small one? That the price is higher for a valuable house than for a wretched hut? Higher for a piano than a wooden stool? Does government price regulation not set a higher price for a great service than for a smaller one? Do consumer cooperatives not sell fine assortments of coffee at a higher price than low grade ones? Sugar higher than flour, and caviar higher than sugar? Does "custom" not set a higher remuneration for a skilled doctor or attorney than for a laborer or street cleaner?

It may be said that such are dull and foregone conclusions. Indeed, foregone conclusions; but they are such only because it is self-evident that considerations of utility and cost are decisive. This is why we can approach the development of a basic law, which reveals the influence of self-interest and desire for exchange gain, with the awareness that we thereby develop that part of the price theory which, among all others, is indispensable for an understanding of price phenomena.

III
THE BASIC LAW OF PRICE

At the outset of this chapter, I would like to submit a few remarks on the basic theme that provides the keystone for this whole analysis.

The decisions that must be made in exchange negotiations always pertain to the following two points: Do we really want to exchange in a given situation? And in case we are inclined to do so, what are the exchange conditions we endeavor to make? It is obvious that someone who merely seeks direct gain in the exchange negotiation will make decisions according to the following rules: (1) *he will exchange only, if the transaction yields gain to him*; (2) *he prefers to exchange at a greater gain than a smaller one;* (3) *he will prefer to exchange at a smaller gain than none at all.*

We need no further clarification of how these three rules reflect our basic motive. But further discussion is in order for the common expression "to exchange at a gain."

It obviously means that the acquired goods yield greater utility for our well-being than the goods given in exchange. In other words, because the significance of goods manifests itself in their subjective value, the acquired goods have a higher subjective value than those given in exchange. If A owns a horse and is to exchange it for 1,000 gallons of wine, he can and will do so only if the offered 1,000 gallons of wine have a greater value for him than his horse. Of course, the exchange partner has similar thoughts. He will forego his 1,000 gallons of wine only, if he receives a good that has a greater value for him. He will want to exchange his 1,000 gallons of wine for the horse of A only, if the wine is worth less to him than the horse.

We may deduce an important principle from this. *An exchange is economically possible only between individuals who attach different, indeed opposing values, to the economic good and medium of exchange.* The buyer must ascribe a higher value to the good than to the medium of exchange, and the seller a lower value. Their interest in exchange and exchange gain becomes greater the greater the difference in their valuation happens to be. When this difference declines, their exchange gain also declines. If, finally, their valuations do not differ at all, if they move in the same direction, an exchange between them then is economically impossible.[1]

It has often been said and also denied that, in a fair exchange, both goods quantities must be equal in value, that they must be "equivalents." It would lead me too far, if I were to pursue in all its details this controversy which I believe to be rather unfortunate and unfruitful.[2] I merely would like to note that, if the word "value" is used in its subjective sense, an equivalence of goods acquired and given in exchange is not only not necessary, but even impossible. For we do not trade, if the exchange affords no gain, and it brings no gain, if the exchange good is worth precisely the good we give in exchange.

After our discussion of subjective value in Part I of this work, we need no longer explain that opposing valuations may occur.[3] But that they must occur frequently in our economic lives follows from our division of labor. Every producer manufactures only a few items in large quantities that exceed his personal demand. He, therefore, has a surplus of *his* product but a scarcity of all other products. He attaches a lower value to his product and a relatively higher subjective value to the other products. The manufacturers of

---

[1] If, for instance, A places the value of his horse at 500 gallons and B at fifteen hundred gallons, then the exchange at one thousand gallons brings each a gain equivalent to the value of five hundred gallons of wine. If A values the horse at eight hundred and B at twelve hundred gallons, the exchange nets each one a gain of the value of only two hundred gallons. If, finally, the valuations of both coincide at twelve hundred gallons, B would be glad to acquire the horse for one thousand gallons or for any price lower than twelve hundred gallons, but A, of course, would not be willing to part with it. Cf. Menger, *Grundsätze der Volkswirtschaftslehre*, p. 155 et seq.

[2] On this controversy cf. Menger, op. cit., p. 173 et seq.; also Neumann in Schönberg's *Handbuch*, 2nd ed., Chapter I, p. 158 *et seq.*

[3] See above, especially p. 44.

the latter, however, attach a higher value to his product which they need, and a lower value to their own products which they have in abundance. The condition of opposing valuation favorable to exchange has thus been met.

Let us pursue yet another thought that springs from the preceding discussion. As we have seen, an exchange is economically possible only, if an individual values the acquired good more highly than that which he offers in exchange. This holds true the lower he values his own good and the higher he values the medium of exchange. The horse owner who attaches a subjective value of $500 to his horse and a value of $100 to a barrel of wine enjoys a greater potential for exchange or, as we shall call it in the future, a greater *exchange capacity* than another owner who values his horse at $1,000 and a barrel of wine at only $50. The former obviously can realize an exchange if only six barrels were offered for his horse, while the latter would have to refuse the exchange if fewer than twenty barrels of wine were offered to him. If a third owner were to attach a value of only $400 to his horse and $150 to a barrel of wine, he would obviously be able to consummate the exchange, even if the price were to decline to three barrels of wine. In general terms, *he who attaches lowest value to his own good in comparison with the good he would like to acquire, or, that is to say, he who attaches the highest value to the other good in comparison with his own good has the greatest exchange capacity.*[4]

After this short discussion of the meaning and content of our basic motive, we may approach our real task: the effects this basic motive have on the formation of price. For this part of our task I would like to adopt a method that was already used by several excellent predecessors. First, I would like to demonstrate through examples how price is determined under certain conditions. Then I would like to isolate the common trait from the examples and,

[4] The term "exchange capacity" which is so fruitful for an explanation of exchange and price phenomena was first used by Menger (*Grundsätze*, p. 186 et seq.) I replaced his term "exchange power" with "exchange capacity" for reasons of terminological suitability.

then formulate the principle.[5]

I would like to begin with a simple typical case, with the formation of price in an isolated exchange between a pair of exchange partners.

A. Formation of Price in an Isolated Exchange

Farmer A needs a horse. He needs it so badly that he values the possession of a horse as much as he values the possession of $300. He goes to his neighbor B who has a horse for sale. If, B ascribes an equal or greater value to the horse as to the possession of $300, then, as we know, no exchange takes place between the two. But let us assume that B attaches a much lower value to the horse, let us say only $100. Now what will happen?

First, an exchange will be made. Under these conditions, both exchange partners can earn a sizeable gain through the exchange. For instance, if they exchange the horse at $200, then A, to whom the desired horse is worth $300, will gain $100, and similarly B, who will receive $200 for a horse which is worth only $100 to him. According to the motto "It is better to exchange with a small gain than not at all," both will agree to the exchange at a price that affords a gain to both. What will the price be?

We may say with certainty: the price must be lower than $300, otherwise, A will have no economic advantage and, therefore, no motive to make the exchange; the price also must be higher than $100, otherwise the exchange will inflict a loss on B or be useless. But it cannot be determined with certainty at which point between $100 and $300 the price will be set. Every price between these two limits is economically feasible– a price of $101 as well as one of $299. There is much leeway for bargaining. It depends on the ability of the buyer or seller to negotiate, on cunning, obstinacy, or

---

[5] Cf. Schäffle's Ges. System, 3rd ed., p. 187 et seq.; also Menger's *Grundsätze*, p. 172-212. As long as 15 years ago Menger presented in an exemplary manner the basic conditions of price determination. It is strange that contemporary price theory has sought to profit little from it. This can perhaps be explained by the circumstance that, in the meantime, the whole theory of "supply and demand," which served his analyses both as support and object for improvement, had fallen in disrepute.

persuasion, etc. whether the price is pushed toward the lower limit or the upper limit. If both partners show equal ability in bargaining, the price will be set approximately in the center, near $200.

Let us briefly summarize what can be stated as a general principle. *In isolated exchange, the price is set within a range the upper limit of which is the subjective valuation by the buyer and the lower limit the valuation by the seller.*

B. Formation of Price with One-sided Competition Among Buyers

Let us vary our example a little and assume that prospective buyer A meets a competitor A_2 who also intends to purchase the horse from owner B. A_2 attaches a value of $200 to the possession of the horse. What will happen now?

Each of the two competitors desires to purchase B's horse, but of course only one will get it. Each one wants to be the buyer. Each one will try to persuade B to sell him the horse. He will do so by bidding a higher price than his competitor. We will witness the common phenomenon of alternate outbidding. For how long? It will go on until the rising price reaches the valuation of the less capable competitor, in our case A_2. As long as the bidding lies under $200 A_2 will be guided by the principle "it is better to exchange at a smaller gain than not at all," and therefore raise his bid. Of course, A_1 will prevent the transaction by raising his bid according to the same motto. But A_2 must not exceed the limit of $200 lest the exchange inflict a loss on him. At this point it is to his advantage "not to exchange at all rather than at a loss" and, therefore, he will yield to his competitor.

This does not mean that A_1 will have to pay a price of $200. It is possible that B, who knows A_1's urgent need for a horse is not satisfied with $200, and manages through obstinacy and bargaining to obtain a price of $250, $280, perhaps even of $299 from A_1. We may be certain, however, that the price cannot exceed $300 (the valuation of successful buyer A), and that it cannot fall below $200 (the valuation of excluded buyer A_2).

Let us assume that in addition to A and A_2, there are three other buyers A_3, A_4, and A_5. They ascribe a value of $220, $250, and $280 to the possession of the horse respectively. As can readily be seen, in the ensuing competition buyer A_3 will raise his bid to the limit of \$220, A_4 to \$250, and A_5 to \$280. And again, the most capable competitor A will prevail and the purchase price will be set between \$300 as the upper limit and \$280 as the lower limit, which is the valuation of the most capable of all excluded competitors.

The results of our analysis may now be stated in general terms: *in the case of one-sided competition of potential buyers, the strongest bidder who values the economic good most highly in comparison with the medium of exchange becomes the buyer. The price moves between the valuation of the buyer as the upper limit and the valuation of the strongest excluded would-be buyer as the lower limit. In addition, there is a second subsidiary lower limit which is always the seller's own valuation.* Comparing these statements with the result of our typical case discussed in Section A, we observe that the competition of buyers tends to reduce the range for price determination; it does so in an upward direction. Between A and B alone, the limits were \$100 and \$300; the addition of other competitors lifted the lower limit to \$280.

C. Formation of Price with One-sided Competition among Sellers

This scenario illustrates the very opposite of the preceding case, i.e., many sellers rather than many buyers. Analogous tendencies lead to analogous results, except that they work in the opposite direction. Our presentation may be brief.

Let us assume that A is the only willing buyer who is confronted with five horse owners B_1, B_2, B_3, B_4, B_5 each of whom offers him a horse (we assume that all horses are of equal quality). B_1's valuation of the horse is \$100, B_2's \$120, B_3's \$150, B_4's \$200, B_5's \$250. Each one of the five competitors wants to make the sale. To prevail over his competitors, each one tries to underbid, as in the preceding case the competing buyers tried to overbid. But since no one is willing to offer his horse for less than it is worth to himself, B_5 will stop underbidding at \$250, B_4 at \$200, B_3 at \$150. Then only B_1 and B_2 will continue to compete with each other until finally, at \$120, B_2 will find himself "economically excluded,"[6] and B_1 alone remains. The selling price must be higher than \$100, otherwise he would gain no advantage and, therefore, lack the

[6] Menger, *ibid.*, p. 183.

motive for exchange. And the price cannot possibly exceed $120, otherwise B_2 would have continued his bidding. Stated in general terms: *in the case of one-sided competition among sellers, it is again the strongest competitor who places upon his own good the lowest valuation in relation to the buyer's offer who consummates the exchange. And the price is set between the valuation of the seller as lower limit, and that of his strongest excluded competitor as upper limit.*[7] In contrast to the case of isolated exchange set forth in section A, where the price was set between $100 and $300, the competition of sellers restricts the range in a downward direction.

D. Formation of Price with Two-sided Competition

The case of two-sided competition is both most frequent in real life and most important for the development of the law of price. We therefore must give it the most thorough attention.

The typical situation which this sort of case presupposes can be represented by the table below. It conveys the picture of ten willing buyers and eight willing sellers each of whom wishes to buy or to sell one horse. At the same time, the table indicates the degree of subjective valuation by each of the candidates for exchange. The irregularity of valuations is in keeping with the actualities of economic life. In fact, individual conditions of supply and demand which determine subjective value vary so widely that any two persons rarely place exactly the same subjective value on any one thing.

---

[7] Of course, this is regardless of the second subsidiary upper limit that is drawn by the buyer's valuation but rarely becomes important in case of extensive competition among sellers.

Willing Buyers	Valuation	Willing Sellers	Valuation
A_1	$300	B_1	$100
A_2	280	B_2	110
A_3	260	B_3	150
A_4	240	B_4	170
A_5	220	B_5	200
A_6	210	B_6	215
A_7	200	B_7	250
A_8	180	B_8	260
A_9	170		
A_{10}	150		

It is necessary to add that all parties are in the same market at the same time, that all the horses offered are equal in quality, and, finally, that all the candidates for exchange are free from any misconception regarding the market situation, which could prevent them from effectively pursuing their interests.[8] Once more we ask, "What happens in this situation?"

A_1, whose individual circumstances cause him to value a horse at $300, considers it to his advantage to buy at a price of $290, and each of the eight sellers are most eager to sell his horse to A_1 at such an advantageous price. But obviously A_1 would be acting rather unwisely, if he were to buy prematurely at so high a price. His advantage demands that he earn not just any profit but a maximum profit. To that end, he refrains from hastily making the highest offer to which he could agree. Instead, he begins with bids that are as low as those of his competitors of lesser capacity for exchange; he will consent to raise his bid only at such time and to such extent as becomes necessary to prevent his exclusion from the exchange.

In similar fashion, B_1 could very well sell his horse for $110

---

[8] If, for instance, a buyer erroneously supposes that the supply delivered to market is materially smaller than actually is the case, he may agree to a higher price than necessary. Of course, the theory of price cannot overlook the influence of such or similar mistakes, but this is not the place to consider them. It is our purpose at this point to develop only the simplest fundamental law.

and could very quickly find buyers at that price. But he will carefully reserve the lowest offer he *could* possibly accept, and will make his offer to sell just low enough to remain in the competition for the sale. The bargaining will therefore presumably begin with restraint, the willing buyers, on the one hand, bidding low prices and the willing sellers, on the other hand, exhibiting the same restraint by demanding high prices.[9]

Let us assume that the buyers begin with a bid of \$130. It is clear that in the absence of some gross error in the understanding of market conditions no sale will be concluded at that price. All ten buyers place the value of a horse at over \$130 and all ten are willing to buy, while only two horses could be offered economically at that price– the horses owned by B_1 and B_2. It is clear that these two sellers would be acting unwisely by failing to exploit the competition among the buyers to bring about a higher price. The buyers would also be acting unwisely if they allowed the most advantageous purchase opportunities to be snatched away by two of their number without making an attempt to offer a somewhat higher and yet very advantageous price. Hence, just as in the case described in Section B, there will have to be a sifting out of the large number of buyers through attempts on their own part to outbid each other. How long will that keep up?

At \$150, all ten buyers can still remain in the bidding. From that point on, the competitors with the least capacity for exchange

---

[9] The more experienced in business and the more familiar with the state of the market the people are who are seeking to do business on the open market, the more quickly they terminate the preliminary "sounding out" by means of reserved or intentionally inadequate bidding. In a market where the action moves in "deep and well-worn grooves" the participants will dispense entirely with extreme bids that have no prospect of acceptance. Their very first offers will at least approach the zone within which the market price will ultimately fall. The extreme instance of abbreviated bidding is "fixed prices" which the sellers set themselves. They represent a renunciation of all "sounding out" bids and are an attempt to predict with complete accuracy the exact zone into which market conditions will set the price. They must attempt to guess that zone accurately. If they set the price lower than the market price zone, an opportunity for gain is lost, and if they set it higher, buyers will fill their needs in the market by patronizing other competitors, and the goods will not be disposed of. "Fixed prices" are less customary in an open market than in shops where sales are never made under the direct pressure of competition and a miscalculation in the asking price is not quite so risky.

must drop out, one after the other. At \$150, A_{10} is forced to drop out, A_9 likewise at \$170, A_8 at \$180, A_7 at \$200. But at the same time, as prices rise, there is an increase in the number of sellers for whom participation in the exchange becomes an economic possibility. From \$150 up, B_3 can give serious thought to making a sale, at \$170, B_4 can do so, and at \$200, B_5 can, too. A shrinkage in the discrepancy between buyers and sellers thus gradually begins. At first, the number of horses desired and the number effectively offered for sale differed widely. At \$130, there was an effective demand for *ten* horses and only *two* could have been economically offered for sale. Now, at a price higher than \$200, there is an effective demand for only *six* horses and *five* are offered for sale. The number of willing buyers exceeds by one the number of competitors able to sell. Nevertheless, as long as the number of buyers is in excess of the number of sellers, and this aspect of the market condition is correctly perceived by all parties, the sales cannot be consummated. For one thing, the sellers still have the possibility of exploiting the excess of competing buyers to increase the price still more, and they have the incentive to do so. For another thing, the conflicting interests of the buyers compel them to continue to outbid each other. A_6 would pursue his interests rather poorly if he allowed his five competitors to buy the five most inexpensive horses "from under his nose." He would have absolutely no chance to make an exchange and hence to gain through such exchange.[10] At the same time, none of A_6's competitors can permit him to acquire one of the five horses offered for sale. If one does, the one who withdraws in A_6's favor, though he could still purchase the horse he needs, would have to get it from among the remaining less favorably priced horses offered by the more stubborn sellers B_6, B_7 and B_8. He would have to pay a price which, *at the least*, exceeds the subjective valuation which B_6 places on his horse and exceeds \$215. The realization of their gain thus impels all the buyers to continue to outbid each

---

[10] Once the sellers B_1 to B_5 have sold their horses, the seller with the greatest capacity for exchange remaining is B_6 whose valuation of his own horse is placed at \$215, which is higher than the valuation of A_5. Hence, as we already know, an exchange between them is economically impossible. The same is true, to an even greater degree, of competitors B_7 and B_8 who have even less capacity for exchange.

other above the $200 mark.

The situation changes significantly when the rising bids reach the $210 mark. A_6 is forced to drop out of the bidding representing "effective demand"; there now are only five bidding buyers opposite five willing sellers. Because the five buyers can be satisfied simultaneously, there is no longer any reason for them to drive each other out of the market by raising their bids. On the contrary, it is IN their common interest to close their transactions at the lowest possible price. The bidding by the buyers, which up to this time prevented a transaction from being closed, now comes to an end. *It is possible* to close at a price of $210.

It does not follow, however, that the closing *must* be at that price. It is possible that the sellers can be stubborn and that, hoping for still higher prices, they refuse an offer of $210. What happens in that case? At first, the willing buyers, lest they fail to accomplish their purpose, will continue to bid. But they are getting close to their limits. If the price demands of the sellers should exceed $220, A_5 would have to forego the purchase and there would then be five willing sellers facing four willing buyers. In that case, one of the sellers would have to drop out. And because nobody wants to be the one to drop out, the overbidding by buyers will give way to *under*bidding by the sellers until the fifth seller has found a buyer. He finds him below the $220 mark.[11]

In fact, in our example the price limit would have to be somewhat lower still. For as long as it were a question of a price exceeding $215, a sixth possible seller would appear in the person of B_6. His appearance would place the sellers in the majority as compared with the five buyers, which would require the sellers to avoid being excluded from the exchange. They would have to underoffer each other. When the weakest party to this competition meets defeat, the issue is settled. That defeat befalls B_6 in the moment when the price demands of the offering sellers fall below $215. At that moment, the number of competitors in the group of sellers becomes equal to the number in the group of buyers and

[11] It is self-evident that the gradual "bidding up" by the willing buyers and the gradual "bidding down" by the sellers do not by any means necessarily take place as two separate and successive stages of the process. Both activities usually occur simultaneously.

price reaches the level at which competition ceases. If we presume economic behavior of all competitors and correct perception of the condition of the market, he zone within which the price must be determined lies between the limits of \$210 and \$215. Only within that zone do we have the situation that meets the two conditions necessary for completion of the transaction. All the parties who are still in a position to "talk business" can at that price gain an advantage. All those who cannot, that is to say, the excluded competitors, have no power to interfere in the business of the others.[12]

Let us cull from this long presentation of the facts those fruits which offer nourishment for our theory of price. We may deduce answers of broad validity to four questions. Two concern the persons of the groups effecting an exchange, two concern the price at which the exchange is made.

Our first question: *Among the competitors seeking to exchange, which ones actually succeed in doing so?* Our example gives us a precise answer: *the competitors in both groups possessing the greatest capacity for exchange.* That is to say, it is the willing purchasers who place the highest value on the good (A_1 to A_5) and the willing sellers who place the lowest value on it (B_1 to B_5).

The second question: *How many competitors on either side consummate an exchange?* The answer to this question is important inasmuch as the definitiveness of the price law depends on the answer. Let us look once more at our example. Five pairs effect an exchange. We note that they are the same five pairs who, regarded individually, meet the economic requirements necessary for an exchange. That is to say, both members of each pair place a higher value on what he is to receive than on that with which he is to part.

---

[12] It is obvious that the result derived in our abstract table more closely approximates actual practice the more completely all participants are cognizant of the market situation as a whole -- in short, the more concentrated the scene of operations and the more complete the publicity. On the other hand, it is usually the case that the operations are carried on under such conditions that the respective groups though able to communicate are nevertheless separated in time or in space. In this case, of course, the competitive conditions applying to the market as a whole are not fully operative within any one group. Consequently, the prices determined within the several groups frequently would only approximate more or less closely the ideal market prices derived by our table.

Those pairs for whom this cannot be said are excluded from accomplishing an exchange. This is no mere fortuitous result but rather a result based on inner necessity.[13] The number of pairs is limited to those that meet the required conditions when we pair them off in descending order of their capacity for exchange. First we pair off the two with the greatest capacity, next those with the second greatest capacity, and so on.[14]

---

[13] In order for A_6, in addition to his competitors A_1 to A_5, to effect an exchange, it is necessary for a sixth seller to appear, one who is willing to offer a horse at a price economically possible for A_6, that is, at less than $210. A_6 is excluded because there is no B_6. And B_6, for his part, is excluded because there is no A_6 who is willing to pay a price economically possible for B_6, namely, one in excess of $215. If we change the figures in our example so that A_6 also puts a higher valuation on a horse than B_6– say one of $216, it can readily be seen that the "bidding up" terminates between $215 and $216 and that A_6 and B_6 become a sixth pair to be included among those actually effecting an exchange.

[14] It is, to be sure, possible to pair off the parties aiming to negotiate an exchange in such fashion as to have no fewer than eight pairs in which each willing buyer places a higher value on the economic good than does the willing seller. Such a pairing appears as follows:

A10	$150	B1	$100
A9	170	B2	110
A8	180	B3	150
A7	200	B4	170
A6	210	B5	200
A5	220	B6	215
A4	260	B7	250
A3	280	B8	260
A2	240		
A1	300		

It is clear that economic behavior of all of the participants precludes exchanges according to this pairing. If B1, for instance, makes an exchange with A10 he would have to be satisfied with a sales price well below A10's valuation, which he certainly will not do since he can get a higher price from any of the other willing buyers. Similarly for A2, to make an exchange with B8, A2 would have to pay a price in excess of $260 which he is not inclined to do, nor is it necessary to do so under prevailing market conditions. But as those willing to make an exchange refuse to deal with those who offer to trade only on unfavorable terms, the latter automatically suffer exclusion, and the number of pairs available to consummate an exchange becomes restricted to that indicated in the text.

(continued...)

We may therefore formulate the general rule as follows: *Pairing off the competitors in descending order of capacity for exchange, the number of pairs making an exchange will be determined by the number of pairs in which the willing buyer places a higher value on the good than does the seller.*

The third and fourth questions concern price directly.

The *third* question leads us to the conclusion that all exchanges effected under the influence of competition at any one given time are consummated *at an approximately uniform price*. We did that in our example where we demonstrated that all five pairs would negotiate their exchanges at prices falling within the range of $210 and $215.

The most important question is the fourth, namely, "Where does the 'market price' find its level?" In no event may it be higher than the valuation by A_5, and in no event may it be lower than the valuation by B_5. Otherwise the price would have been so high that the fifth buyer would have been excluded, or it would have been so low as to exclude the fifth seller. And with either one excluded, no price is established. But it is also true that the price could in no event be higher than the valuation by B_6 nor lower than that of A_6. Otherwise there would have been an addition of a sixth bidder to the ranks of willing buyers or of a sixth competitor to the ranks of willing sellers. And again, the price would not have been determined and there would have been no escape from the over- and under-bidding until the price had been forced within the range already noted.

Let us couch this conclusion in general terms. Where there is two-sided competition, the market price will find its *level* at a point within a range having an upper and a lower limit. The upper limit is determined by the valuation by the last buyer to come to terms and the valuation by that excluded willing seller who has the greatest capacity for exchange. The lower limit is determined by the valuation of the last seller among those coming to terms and the valuation of that excluded willing buyer who has the greatest capacity for exchange. This double limitation thus sets the narrow

---

[14] (...continued)

range.[15] Now let us discard the cumbersome and detailed description of the four persons described as the price-determining factors and employ the short and descriptive term of "marginal pairs." We arrive at the following law of price: the market price is limited and determined by the subjective value judgments of both marginal pairs of buyers and sellers.[16]

Notice that the analogy between the determination of price and that of subjective value is rather striking. The subjective value of a good is a "marginal value" which is determined by the last utility at which a good can be economically employed. This is true regardless of the more important uses to which individual units of the total supply may be devoted. In the same way, every market price is a "marginal price" and is limited by the economic condition of those competing pairs that are situated at the very limit or margin of the "capacity for exchange." It can also readily be seen that this analogy is no coincidence but rather an example of related causes bringing about related results. In the case of subjective valuation, the motive of economic gain demanded that the available goods supply must be utilized to satisfy wants in a descending order of their importance, the marginal as the last. In the formation of price, the motive of economic gain of the participants assures

[15] In our example, the deciding factor is the valuations by the excluded contracting parties A_6 and B_6. However, if the valuations of A_6 had been only $190 instead of $210, and if that of B_6 had been $230 instead of $215, the limits of the range within which the price would be set would have been the valuations of the last pair actually effecting an exchange. In other words, the price would have had to have been set between $200 and $220.

[16] A few remarks of minor significance may well be assigned to this footnote. It is very easy to see that two-sided competition, in comparison with isolated exchange, tends to produce a limited price range within which the contracting parties are free to move. This range is limited from both directions. If A1 and B1, for instance, were dealing in an isolated exchange, they could have come to terms anywhere inside the wide range of $100 to $300. But now they, and all the other contracting parties as well, are forced into that very limited range which is all that remains open between the valuations by the marginal pairs. Furthermore, it can now be seen why we had to find a definite answer to the question of how many pairs of competitors actually consummate an exchange. If that number were indefinite or a matter of chance, the persons who constitute our marginal pairs would also be indefinite and our whole law of price, which derives its formula from the economic situation of those particular persons, would likewise be indefinite.

that the pairs of contracting parties with the greatest capacity for exchange consummate the exchanges in descending order, again with the "marginal pair" as the last. In the former case, gratification was assured to all wants that possess greater importance than the marginal utility; it was assured even without the unit on which the final or marginal utility depends. In the latter case, consummation of an exchange, at higher or lower prices, was assured to all pairs of contracting parties possessing greater exchange capacity than the marginal pair. Only the fate of the last or marginal pair depends on whether the price reaches a certain point, either high or low. And finally, just as the importance of the last dependent want lends its value to an economic good by virtue of this relationship of dependence, so do the economic circumstances of the last pair of contracting parties dictate the price of a good.

In this connection I would like to call attention to an interesting fact. I hope that this fact will lend support to our theory in the eyes of knowledgeable theorists. These very ideas with which we endeavor to explain the whole determination of value and price have already found acceptance in our literature, especially in the solution of value and price problems. Von Thünen taught that the rate of capital interest is determined by the productivity of the "*last* unit of capital invested," and that the height of wages is determined by the productivity of the "*last* worker employed in an enterprise." Much earlier, the question, "Which among several costs rules the market price?" was answered "the highest production costs still necessary for the needed market supply." In other words, the "last seller" was the correct answer. All these answers constitute special cases of the same principle on which we have built the doctrine of marginal utility and the theory of price. Unfortunately, the authors were unaware of the universal significance of their new ideas. They intended to develop a few special rules with limited significance. In reality, they struck upon the "main theme" that is used for the pursuit of economic interests and thus also the formation of value and price.

The relations between price and subjective value by no means exhaust the foregoing analogy. It is of greater significance that *price, from beginning to end, is the product of subjective valuations*. Let us retrace our mental steps. It is the relation between the subjective valuations placed upon the good and its medium of exchange that determines who can enter the competition to exchange the one for the other. That same relation determines the capacity for exchange. It establishes exactly for every participant the point up to which his economic advantage demands that he continue to compete and, just as exactly, the limit that forces him to concede defeat and withdraw to the ranks of those who have been outbid and thus excluded. Furthermore, that relation also determines who, among the competitors possessing the "greatest capacity for exchange," shall consummate an exchange; it determines who shall occupy the position of marginal pair, and it ultimately determines how high the price shall be at which the actual exchange takes place. Hence, throughout the entire pricing process –insofar as it takes place on the basis of self-regarding motivations– there is not a single phase, not a single feature which cannot be traced back to the subjective valuation of an economic good and its medium of exchange as the underlying cause. We therefore describe price as *the resultant of subjective valuations facing each other in the market place.*

It is, to be sure, a resultant of a peculiar kind. Price does not derive simply from the sum or from the average of all valuations made. These valuations exert quite a variety of influences on price. A certain portion of them, namely the valuations of the excluded competitors, exert no influence at all, with the single exception of that excluded pair which possesses the greatest capacity for exchange. As to the others, it would make no difference, if ten times as many of them were represented in the market, the result would not change one iota. In our own example, the excluded competitors A_7, A_8, A_9, and A_{10} may or may not be present in the market. The category of those "excluded" might be represented by those four or by hundreds of additional competitors. They are all competition who are not in the position to bid more than $200 for a horse. In any case, price will inevitably be determined, as before, at a point between $210 and $215. The excluded competitors can swell the market crowd, but they are no market factor when determinating price.[17]

---

[17] We are assuming that the competitors appearing in the market have an accurate understanding of the market situation. Without that assumption it would, (continued...)

There is a second group that plays a very peculiar role. This is the group of valuations made by all the pairs of contracting parties actually consummating an exchange, excepting the last pair. They check and neutralize each other. Let us look once more at our typical example. If we seek the effect A's presence has on price, we discover that it offsets one member of the opposing group, B_1; it does this so effectively that the pricing process goes on in exactly the same way as if A_1 and B_1 were not present at all. Similarly, we can see that A_2, A_3 and A_4 cancel the effectiveness of the opposing B_2, B_3 and B_4. With all of them present, the price is determined at a point between \$210 and \$215. If all of them were absent, A_5 and B_5 would exchange at a price between \$210 and \$215. Please note that the subjective valuations of this group are a matter of complete indifference. For instance, A_1 ascribing a value of \$300 completely neutralizes B_1 if B_1 places a value of only \$250 or even \$220. Inversely, even if A's valuation were \$2,000 or \$20,000, this fantastically high number does not affect the price either. Its entire effectiveness is still completely absorbed in its neutralization of B_1.

Even though the valuations by this group may lack *any direct influence* on price, we can not say that they exert no influence whatsoever. The valuations that belong to this group –in our table those by A_1, A_2, A_3 and A_4– by neutralizing the valuations made by an equal number of the opposing group –our B_1, B_2, B_3, B_4– serve a double purpose. In the first place, they prevent a stronger seller than B_5 from becoming half of the marginal pair which directly determines the price. Moreover, they prevent a situation in which the strongest sellers, being offset no longer, can neutralize the next strongest buyers and thus allow some still weaker buyers, instead of A_5, to participate in the determinative marginal pair.[18] We can,

---

[17] (...continued)
to be sure, be possible that the presence of a hundred potential buyers might lead to the mistaken notion that their number included a sizeable group possessing high capacity for exchange. Such a situation might mislead the few competitors present who actually possess such capacity into making premature price offers that are excessively high.

[18] To demonstrate this, let us omit competitors A_1, A_2, A_3 and A_4 from our example altogether. The position of the remaining parties is as follows:

(continued...)

therefore accurately formulate the role played by all those exchanging pairs whose capacity for exchange exceeds that of the marginal pair. We can do so precisely in the following words: they exert no direct influence on the determination of price by their valuations; but they do exert an indirect influence insofar as they reserve the position of marginal pair to some other pair by their reciprocal neutralization.

Finally, there is a third and very small group of valuations that play a conclusive and deciding role in the determination of price. That group comprises the valuations of the marginal pair. They and they alone are the forces that directly influence a market price. All weaker competitors attempting to effect an exchange, are without influence on price; all stronger competitors neutralize each other; only the marginal pairs remain. At first glance, it may seem odd that so few persons, and particularly persons so lacking in prominence, can make the decision that governs the fate of the whole market. But a closer examination will reveal this to be perfectly natural. If all are to exchange at *one and the same* market price, that price must be set to suit *all* persons who make the exchange. Now every price that suits the contracting parties possessing the least capacity for exchange must naturally suit all persons with greater capacity for exchange in correspondingly

---

[18] (...continued)

A_5	\$220	B_1	\$100
A_6	210	B_2	110
A_7	200	B_3	150
A_8	180	B_4	170
A_9	170	B_5	200
A_{10}	150	B_6	215
		B_7	250
		B_8	260

It is apparent that now the last pair representing a range within which an exchange is permitted is the pair A8 and B4. The member of the marginal pair representing the buyers now is in a much weaker economic position than was the case before; the competitive sellers are represented in the marginal pair by a much stronger representative. Accordingly, the limits of the price range which formerly stood at \$210 and \$215 now move downwards touching \$170 and \$180 respectively.

greater degree. But we cannot add "and vice versa"! And for that reason the economic situations of the *last pair* to whom the price is acceptable, or of the first pair to whom it is not acceptable, must necessarily set the price.

This leads us to an important conclusion. Every change in the relation of both exchanging parties, that is, in "the relation of supply and demand," need not lead to a change in the market price. On the contrary, all those changes that fail to disturb the solely decisive marginal pairs remain without influence. Let us state that in greater detail: any increase or decrease in the number of *excluded competitors* is irrelevant; every increase or decrease in the *valuation on the part of these persons* is likewise irrelevant, provided it is not of such magnitude that they cease to be "excluded" competitors. And, finally, every increase or decrease, (even a unilateral one), in the *valuation on the part of competitors actually effecting an exchange*--except for the marginal pair--is also irrelevant provided that such persons are not thereby removed from the ranks of effective buyers and sellers.[19] Only two kinds of change are really significant. One is a change in the valuations by the *marginal pair*; the other is a unilateral change in the *number of persons whose capacity for exchange exceeds that of the marginal pair*. These changes offset prices because they exclude one or more competitors and thus have an impact on the marginal pairs.

All this makes us question the relationship between the price law we developed for two-sided competition and the three other formulations of law pertaining to isolated exchange and one-sided competition. Must we deal with four independent laws governing no fewer than four different varieties of price phenomena? No. The last version includes all earlier versions. It is the most complete and basic version of the law but stated in simplified form befitting the somewhat simplified, yea, stunted circumstances. Because some of the price-determining elements are entirely lacking, the number of price limits declines. But all those price-determining elements that

[19] It makes no difference for the determination of price whether, among a hundred buyers of a commodity which is on sale for $10, there are five or ten individuals who would buy it at a price of $100 or $1,000. Nor would it make any difference, if those same individuals were willing to go no higher than $20. Their readiness to do either is never put to the test.

are present exert their influence in exactly the same way as they do in the principal formulation.[20]

Let us review. Of all the results we have attained in this chapter, the one that is by far of greatest import is the conclusion that all the influences on price have been resolved into *subjective valuations and their rational appreciation*. This is the center of our discussion. If our conclusion is accepted, then the details of our presentation can hardly be questioned. If it is rejected, all the details by themselves lose their convincing force. I may be justified therefore in adding a few more words to the defense of the basic proposition, even though I may already have done so in abundance.

I do really believe that we have hit upon the simplest and most natural and, indeed, the most productive manner of conceiving exchange and price. I refer to the pricing process as a resultant derived from all the valuations that are present in society. This is no analogy, it is living reality. There are genuine *forces* in the pricing process--no physical forces, of course, but psychological. They are the *desires* which those wishing to buy harbor for an economic good and which those wishing to sell have for the money to be obtained for the good. Naturally, the intensity of this force is determined by the benefits which the individual promises himself from the desired good--that is to say, by the (absolute) degree of the subjective *value* which his valuation accords it. The market is the place where the desire for goods belonging to others may be legally translated into effective action. But these forces cannot go into action without restraint, for each is accompanied by a certain *inhibition*. That inhibition consists in the desire to retain possession of what is one's own. The exchange goods of others cannot be acquired without parting with something of one's own. The more difficult it is to take this step, the stronger is the inhibition toward the former. The intensity of the inhibition, of course, reflects the

[20] Let us follow this through for one of the three cases, that of one-sided competition. The buyer meets here the only successful pair, the upper marginal pair. Of the lower marginal pair, there is left only one half, the excluded buyer. Since the influence of the nonexistent excluded competing seller is entirely absent, there are three limits to the range within which the price may be set. These are (1) the value of the good to the effective buyer; (2) its value to the seller; and (3) its value to the excluded buyer possessing the greatest capacity for exchange. And that corresponds exactly to what we have demonstrated in the test above.

importance of the good to be parted with, that is to say, the ranking of its subjective value.

All that follows is quite simple. Competitors who have the smallest capacity for exchange feel the inhibition to be stronger than the force which therefore can exert no effective influence. These individuals neither effect an exchange nor can they exert any influence on the conditions under which others consummate exchanges. In the case of competitors with a greater capacity for exchange, the eagerness with which the goods of others are sought is stronger than the desire to retain what is theirs -- the force is greater than the inhibition. There remains an excess of force which leads to an actual transfer of goods. Now this very excess of force, which is greatest in the competitors possessing the greatest capacity for exchange, would in and of itself be capable of influencing the determination of price. But this perfectly understandable interest of the competitors having greater exchange capacity does not induce them to offer as much as they possibly can. They may offer barely as much as they *must* to succeed. They "succeed" in this case, if they force out competitors and thus assure for themselves a place in the ranks of those effectively consummating an exchange. They, therefore, deliberately refrain from setting in motion the full force of their superior power to force an exchange, and are content to do just enough to maintain their superiority over their closest competitor. It thus is a perfectly natural result that the standard for the determining price is derived from the economic situation of the last of the "ousters" and the first of the "ousted" or, as we expressed it earlier, from the subjective valuations by the marginal pairs.

Orthodox economics has been teaching for centuries that the market price of all goods is determined by the *relation between supply and demand*. Up to this point, I have conscientiously avoided the use of those two terms. What do they mean? Did I merely substitute different words for the same material? Or is it that our law uses not only different terminology but also different content?

I owe an answer to these natural and proper questions. I intend to furnish it with clarity and detail in a special section. But I would like first to add a needed clarification to our law of price, which will both complete my answers and develop our subject matter.

Orthodox economics could hardly be satisfied with its statement that price is determined by the relation of demand and supply. However, it always felt called upon to search for the "deeper causes." In the same way we must not rest with the formula that price is determined by the intersecting valuations of the marginal pairs. We must seek more knowledge of those factors that determine whether this intersection, and thus price, will be on a high or low level. The following section deals with these discussions, and the section thereafter with the relationship between our price law and the law of supply and demand.

IV

THE INDIVIDUAL DETERMINANTS OF PRICE

The preceding chapter established that price is determined by the valuations of the marginal pairs. But we must still *determine whether these valuations are high or low.*

At first, the answer to this question appears to be simple. It is obvious immediately that both the *quantity* of valuations and the intensity of the manifested wants will influence the position of the original pairs. It will work out in the following manner. The price of the marginal pairs will be at a relatively high level when valuations on the part of buyers are very high and relatively numerous while the sellers' valuations are simultaneously low and relatively few in number. In such cases the small number of valuations on the part of the sellers is neutralized by some of the more numerous high valuations on the part of the buyers; the individuals from either group who finally constitute the marginal pairs must necessarily ascribe a high value. For entirely analogous reasons, the valuations will be low when few buyers attach a high value while, at the same time, many sellers attach a low value. These considerations appear again and again in all price theories, illustrated in somewhat different form and graphically in all detail, so that we may proceed without further delay.

If we dissect the individual factors which determine the level of the marginal pairs, we will find the following four "determinants" of price.

1. The number of wants that apply to the good.

2. The valuations on the part of the buyers.

3. The quantity of the commodity that is for sale.

4. The valuations on the part of sellers.

At this point, we can appreciate the full significance of one circumstance mentioned in preceding discussions. I did not emphasize it because such emphasis was not required. I refer to the fact that our "valuation figures" are not just simple quantities. They are by no means simple expressions of the absolute magnitude of the subjective value which the good possesses for the evaluating person. On the contrary, they are *figures expressing relativity* and are derived from the comparison of two different valuations -- one that is applied to the good and one that is applied to the medium of exchange. Let us refer to our schematic example again. When we said that one buyer valued a horse at $200, we did not say anything concerning the absolute significance which the possession of a horse possesses for the well-being of that buyer; we did no more than express the relativity between the value of the horse and the value of the money, its medium of exchange. What we said was that *A* values a horse two hundred times more than he values a dollar. If we are to broach our present problem, that is, the *elementary* factors of the establishment of price, we shall have to eliminate the complex quantities of "valuation figures" and substitute their composite elements. There are two such elements. The first is the absolute rank of the subjective value of the good for the individual ascribing the value; the second is the corresponding absolute rank of subjective value of the medium of exchange. These two elements quite clearly combine their influences in this manner: the higher the absolute value of the good and the lower that of the medium of exchange, the higher will be the valuation figure. And vice versa, of course.

This leads to several deductions too important to pass by. A high valuation figure does not by any means necessarily permit us to infer that a high valuation is placed upon the economic good. It is possible that it results from a low valuation of money. For instance, the valuation figure 200 makes its appearance if someone values a horse at 2000, and one dollar at 10 units of some ideal scale, or if he values the horse at only 20, and one dollar at only one-tenth of such a unit. And that allows us to conclude that the competing buyers with the greatest capacity for exchange, who place the "highest valuation" on the good, do not necessarily coincide with the individuals for whom the desired good possesses the greatest significance for well-being. Indeed, their numbers consist partly of persons actually in great need of the good and partly of persons whose need is not at all pressing but for whom money has but very small value. The converse may hold true among the sellers. The competitors in that group who have the greatest capacity for exchange may include not only individuals who can very easily dispense with the trade good, but also those for whom the economic good has a high value but whose need for money is still more pressing.

This leads us to another remarkable conclusion. We remember that both parties of an exchange must achieve a gain that equals the value difference between the goods given and the goods received. Of course, the gain is all the greater the greater this value difference. Unhampered competition allows competitors *with the greatest value difference* actually to make the exchange. In other words, those buyers who attach the highest value to the desired good when compared with the medium of exchange, and those sellers who ascribe lowest value to the good when compared with the price received are the ones who make the exchange. Therefore, it seems that self-interest in the market place automatically and unwittingly assures achievement of highest possible exchange gains and thus the greatest total gain for the economic well-being of society. There is, so it seems, economic harmony between the individual interests of the successful traders and the common interest of society.

This thought was expressed repeatedly in the remarkable writings of Schäffle on the formation of price. He maintains that the "natural exchange value," as it emerges in the market with "normal economic competition," equates supply and demand "most usefully" and *"socially most beneficially," and thus "provides the greatest quantity of pure utility."*[1]

---

[1] *Gesellschaftliches System der menschlichen Wirtschaft*, 3rd ed., p. 184 *et seq.*, especially pp. 189 and 194. Similarly Walras, *Theorie mathématique de la richesse sociale*, Lausanne, 1883, p.23; also Launhardt, *Mathematische Begründung der Volkswirtschaftslehre*, Leipzig, 1885, p. 30 *et seq.* It seems to me that also his mathematical presentation does not go to the bottom line. I cannot here enter into an analysis of details hidden in complicated mathematical formulae which, when taken out of context, would be unintelligible to the reader. I just would like to remark that the writings of the "mathematical school" contain many interesting and sagacious discussions which, however, lack the clarity of Menger. Their development of concepts is especially unfortunate, for which the

(continued...)

No matter how appealing this opinion is, it is nevertheless misleading. It rests on a confusion of *relative* and *absolute* exchange gains. It is true, under the influence of unhampered competition the greatest number of dollars is earned. Goods are moving into the hands of those competitors who, in terms of dollars, value the goods more highly than money, that is, those competitors who gain the greatest relative exchange advantage as measured by price. But a great relative exchange gain can, under certain circumstances, be a very modest absolute gain. This is the case, if the monetary unit measuring the exchange gain has a low subjective value for the individual.

A concrete example may illustrate the case. Let us assume that buyer A1 in our earlier story is a rich man who is blessed abundantly with material goods. He now wishes to add another horse to the dozen luxury horses already in his stable. Because his desire concerns a want that is easily foregone, its fulfillment has very little significance for his well-being. The thirteenth horse thus has very little subjective value, which on an ideal scale may be designated with the number 30. Because our man is abundantly blessed with goods and money, the monetary unit also holds very little value according to the well-known principle of marginal utility. Let us assume that the value of one dollar to him is $^{1}/_{10}$ of our ideal unit. The desired thirteenth horse then will be valued at \$300. If he is able to buy the horse at, let us say \$212, he will earn an impressive \$88 when expressed in money, but only a modest eight and eight tenths ($8\ ^{8}/_{10}$) when measured on our ideal scale.

Let us also assume that buyer A_3 is a farmer who urgently needs a horse for cultivating his land. Naturally, possession of the

---

[1] (...continued)
mathematical form is of little use. Also Launhardt (*ibid*, pp. 1 and 11) "value" is identical with "usefulness."

By the way, it is remarkable that the German Launhardt refers exclusively to the writings of Walras and Jevons. But the very ideas that give such great significance to the works of these scholars and, especially, to the "value equation" so appreciated by Launhardt (ibid, p. 12) were presented long ago in German by Menger (*Grundsätze der Volkswirtschaftslehre*, 1871) in non-mathematical form and their originality, but with greater clarity.

horse for A_3 has incomparably greater well-being significance than A_1's acquisition of the thirteenth luxury horse. Let us designate this significance with the number 130. Because money, too, has a higher value for the less affluent farmer than for the rich man –let us say, one-half of our ideal value unit– the horse is worth a smaller sum of money despite its greater absolute value, that is, \$260. If he can buy the horse at the general market price of \$212, he gains \$48 in terms of money –slightly more than one-half of the rich man's gain– but 24 units of effective welfare gain, which is nearly three times more than 8 $^8/_{10}$. We thus may observe that the greater relative exchange gain can be the smaller gain in absolute terms, and that the smaller relative exchange gain can be the greater gain in absolute terms.

In this example we compared two competitors who both succeeded in making exchanges. But this very relationship of value figures and absolute exchange gain may develop also between a victorious competitor and one eliminated by him, for instance between A_1 and A_6. Let us imagine A_6 as a dirt farmer who needs a horse even more urgently than A_3 but whose valuation of money is even greater because of his poverty. Let us also assume that the value figures are 630 for the horse and three ideal units for the dollar. This corresponds to a money value of \$210 for the horse. But if the influence of competitor A_1 raises the market price to \$212, then A_6 cannot buy– he is excluded economically. But if A_1 does not bid at all, other market conditions being equal, the price is set between \$200 and \$210, let us say, at \$205. And A_6 could purchase a horse. He does so with an exchange gain of \$5 when expressed in money, and 15 units on our ideal value scale. In other words, to satisfy an unimportant luxury want, rich A_1 precluded poor A_6 from trading by placing a higher money bid. To secure the smaller well-being gain of 8 $^8/_{10}$ units, he prevented the greater gain of 15 units. His bid thus inflicted *social harm.*[2]

It is unfortunate that such cases occur frequently in economic life. Instead of offering numerous examples, I would like to present only one that is especially shocking and well-known. In a famine

---

[2] It must be borne in mind that in case of sale to A_6 the exchange gain of the seller would be lower by a few dollars. If the value of the dollar is not very high for him, the utility balance in the text remains the same.

year in Ireland, the nourishing grains, rye, and wheat, are exported in huge quantities, much of which is used to satisfy luxury wants, such as pastry, whisky, etc. At the same time, the poor people of Ireland who cannot afford the market price driven up by the competition of the rich subsist on a miserable potato diet or perish en masse from starvation diseases. Every objective observer will see at first glance that, in this case, exchange competition certainly did not lead to a distribution of wheat and rye that yielded the highest pure utility for preservation of life and betterment of people. And yet, the economic goods fell into the hands of those individuals whose valuation exceeded that of the poor people by the greatest number of "shillings" and "guineas."[3]

Let us resume our subject matter. If we substitute the component elements of which the "valuation figures" are composed, we derive the following *six* determinants of price.

1. *The number of demands that are directed toward the good.*
2. *The absolute rank of the subjective value of the good for the buyers.*
3. *The absolute rank of the subjective value of the medium of exchange for the buyers.*
4. *The quantity of the good offered for sale.*
5. *The absolute rank of the subjective value of the good for the sellers.*

[3] Many a reader may be tempted to accuse me of a contradiction. I said above (p. 109.) that every exchange leads to a genuine gain of well-being springing from the difference in valuation of economic good and medium of exchange. It is all the greater, the greater the valuation difference. But now I am confronting this difference with welfare enhancement, and contend that possibly the greatest difference may correspond to smaller welfare gain, and vice versa. There is no contradiction. In my earlier discussions I always had in mind valuations of the same individuals, in my later discussions those of different individuals. It may be said without hesitation that if A gains a valuation difference of $15, he gains more in money and economic well-being, than if he were to gain only $10. Both figures refer to the same value unit, which is the value one dollar has for A. But it obviously cannot be said that if A gains $15, this may be more in subjective value than $10 earned by someone else. It is possible that the greater amount refers to a smaller unit and, therefore, may represent a smaller total sum than the smaller sum of money.

6. *The subjective value of the medium of exchange for the sellers.*

To complete our explanation of price phenomena, we must take another step and inquire into the "determinants" of our determinants. *What are the actual circumstances that cause buyers and sellers to ascribe a high or low value to an economic good and medium of exchange?*

The answer to this question must be sought exclusively in the subjective value theory, which constitutes the very foundation of the price theory. Because we are already familiar with that theory, I merely need to review it and provide the connection with the task at hand. At some point, however, difficulties will arise necessitating further investigation.

Let us consider our determinants one after another.

1. *The Number of Demands Directed Toward the Good.*

Little can be said concerning this factor that would not be self-evident. It obviously is affected on the one hand by the extensiveness of the market and on the other hand by the character of the want, that is to say, whether or not the good is the object of wide and general want and whether or not its consumption is of such a nature that the good calls for a very large number of units thereof. Articles of clothing are always required in greater number than are Sanskrit grammars. Bread and meat are needed daily and are the subject of more numerous demands than are knives which last several years.

Furthermore, and this is the only observation of theoretical interest called for at this point, not every person whose want engenders the wish to possess an economic good becomes a potential buyer thereof. One needs not only the desire to possess the good, but also the desire to exchange possession of the good for possession of the medium of exchange. And that desire, as we know, exists only when there is an intense desire to acquire the good and a lack of desire to retain the medium of exchange. Countless persons who need a good and wish to possess it nevertheless voluntarily stay out of the market because their valuation of the medium of exchange so far exceeds their valuation of the good. Thus any economic possibility of consummating a purchase is out of the question for them. The roster of those desiring a good constitutes our broadest original register of prospects. A preliminary sifting takes place based on the first two determinants of price, namely, the valuations of the good and of the medium of exchange. The resulting and much reduced classification of persons seriously intending to buy is now subjected to a second sifting. This sifting is the exchange contest itself. Out of it comes the still smaller classification of *effective buyers*.

Although the presence of individuals who never had any serious intention of becoming buyers has at the start no influence at all on the determination of price, their existence cannot be ignored by economic theory. There is no firm barrier setting them apart from the serious potential buyers, and both groups are constantly merging into each other. All the factors that promote the mere "I wish I had" to a serious intention to buy are rather unstable. These factors include the valuation of the good, the corresponding valuation of the medium of exchange, and the presumptive market situation. A very slight change among them may attract new active purchasers into the market. Time and again someone goes to the stock market to sell securities, changes his mind and becomes a buyer, if it looks like prices will rise.

2. *The Valuation of the Good by the Buyers.*

As we know,[4] the measure of value in general is determined by the marginal utility the buyer derives from the good to be acquired. And that marginal utility in turn is determined by the *relation between want and satisfaction*. More explicitly, it is determined, on the one hand, by the number and importance of the wants which demand satisfaction and, on the other hand, by the number of available units of the good, that is, by the degree of relative scarcity. The more comprehensive and important the category of want and the rarer the economic good, the higher the subjective valuation of the buyers tends to be.

At this point we must be mindful of yet another circumstance. There are cases in which the value of a good is not determined by its own immediate marginal utility but by the marginal utility of *goods of a different category* that can be drawn upon as substitutes.

---

[4] Cf. the first part of this essay, especially pp. 32 and 43.

One outstanding example is substitution by way of exchange. Assuming an open market, I do not value my one and only winter overcoat according to its extremely high marginal utility which it yields as a preserver of my health and my life. Instead, assuming I can buy a replacement at any time for $400, I place a value on it of $400 dollars. In such a case, the number of determining factors for the indirect marginal utility tends to increase. As we pointed out before, they are (1) the *market price of the substitution unit*, and (2) the subjective conditions of demand and supply in *the goods category from which the substitution unit is drawn.*[5]

This gives rise to a serious theoretical difficulty. The factor "value of the good for the buyer" may possibly be divided into two elements. One is the supply conditions in *other* want and good categories. The other is identical –in an embarrassing manner– with the market price. I said "in an embarrassing manner." It seems that our explanation is enmeshed in a vicious circle as we explain the market price starting with the buyer's subjective value of the good and then explain the buyer's subjective value starting with the market price. At any rate, the price theory is expected to explain fully this difficulty. We must reproach the older theory for not even attempting an explanation.[6]

In reality, the case is as follows. Knowing for certain that a winter overcoat can be bought for $400, a man values it according to the presumed cost of acquisition rather than its direct marginal utility which may amount to ten times that much. In doing so, he bases his valuation on a provisional assumption that cannot become a reality until he gets to the market. Of course, this makes his valuation conditional and hypothetical. Valuations of this kind are rather numerous in economic life. A newly built factory may be appraised at $100,000 in anticipation of its future returns. A share of bank stock may be valued at $500, while a lottery ticket that may win $100,000, but will probably win nothing, is valued at $10

[5] Cf. pp. 40 f., 43 f.

[6] Rau (*Volkswirtschaftslehre*, 8th ed., section 147) enumerates blithely and without a word of explanation the "exchange value" of the good for the buyer among the determinants of price. And Hermann (*Staatswirtschaftliche Untersuchungen*, 1st ed., p. 74) names equally naively "the other costs of acquisition," which means, he explains, price out of price.

because of the uncertain chance to win. The basis of all such valuations is a more or less uncertain future event that is anticipated.[7]

This fact exerts a very natural influence on the practical application of such valuations. As long as the expected result lies in the future, our anticipation provides a rational, indeed usually the only basis for both our valuation and our actions. But after the events have actually taken place our anticipations are set aside, and our valuations based thereon are withdrawn. We would not dream of letting them to continue guiding our actions. After the day of the lottery, no one will want to pay $10 for the losing ticket or sell his winning ticket for $10.

In our case of the winter coat, the valuations are rather similar. It is quite rational and purposeful to value the coat at only $400 and act accordingly. One might even give it away, assuming a replacement coat is available at $400. It is quite rational for people to rely on assumptions and expectations regarding the price of a goal under all circumstances *except when the price has already been determined in the market.* In the face of reality, anticipation ceases to be the guiding star for our action. He who follows his preconceived opinion on price even though it changes right before his eyes, acts irrationally. He acts like the person who believes that it will rain tomorrow and walks around with an open umbrella even though the sky is blue. In reality, people do not act like that. Subjective valuations of this kind exert no more influence on economic action and market prices than does the general hope to purchase a needed good at a certain price. If we get it at that price -- fine. If not, we cannot just give up; we must dismiss our disappointment and decide whether to bid higher prices *under the new circumstances*.

Our decision depends on whether our market is the only one for the needed goods. If it is the only one, we will, of course, continue to bid and, if necessary, bid up to the level of direct marginal utility which we expect to reap from the good. Failure to buy here and now means not buying at all and foregoing all the direct marginal

---

[7] Cf. my essay on "Rights and Relationships," Innsbruck, 1881, p. 80 - 89, on such estimates.

utility. If we miss the only opportunity to buy the needed winter coat we will freeze and perhaps fall ill. Therefore, in accordance with the motto "it is better to exchange at a small gain than not at all," we agree to any price below the direct marginal utility rather than miss the purchase entirely. To state the conclusion for our price theory, people contribute to the determination of price, not on the basis of the indirect lower marginal utility that assumes a given market price, but according to the higher direct marginal utility because prices are constantly fluctuating.

The situation may be quite different if we have access to several markets. We may cling to the expectation to buy the good at a certain price even though we were disappointed in the first market. We may decide to leave it rather than pay more than expected. In this case, it is our hypothetical valuation that guides our behavior. But it must be emphasized that our behavior is guided in such a way only in the *first* market, not in the market in general. For it is obvious that we would continue our bidding up to the full level of our direct marginal utility before we withdraw from the second market or, if more are open, from the last market. Our hypothetical valuation may cause us to move from market to market, but it cannot suppress the full impact of the direct marginal utility on some part of the entire market. It affords us the general hope to purchase the good economically even though we do not get it at our preconceived valuation. In fact, such hope may cause us again and again to turn to another market. If our hope is disappointed again, we raise our bids rather than forego the purchase entirely.

This leads us to the following result. Subjective valuations based on the supposition that the good can be purchased at a certain price furnish a rule of conduct. But the rule is at best only a psychological guide for our behavior and *never the ultimate standard for action*. That standard is based upon the *good's direct marginal utility*. We thus reach a logical and considered conclusion that is important for our theory. We conclude that the final determinant of price is based upon the relationship of demand and supply of the potential buyers and sellers. We were not enmeshed in a vicious circle or lead astray.

There is another type of case that reveals a certain kinship with the one just discussed. It is the case of the purchaser who does not judge the good for its use value, but rather for its (subjective) exchange value. This is always true when a good is bought for resale. The grain merchant, for instance, who buys wheat from the farmer, or the banker who buys securities on the stock exchange ascribes value solely in accordance with what he hopes to realize from them in another market (after allowing for whatever shipping and handling charges he has incurred). In such transactions, the price determinants follow the following causal sequence. At first, the market price is influenced by the *dealer's appraisal*, which is based on an assumed *price in a second market*; and the latter, in turn, is based on the valuations by potential buyers in the second market area. Hence, through the dealer, the public's valuation in a second market, or the supply and demand in that market, exerts an influence on the price in the first market.

This is hardly surprising. The appearance of a dealer in a market is in fact nothing more than the reflection of the demand of persons who are in a different market area. The function of the dealer may be compared to that of a business agent without directions or orders. He considers the demands of a few dozen or a few hundred absent customers and computes what price they would likely agree to under the prevailing conditions. Then, without their knowledge but for the conduct of their economy, he consummates the purchase within his price range. As far as the determination of price in a given market is concerned, it simply makes no real difference whether a dealer buys 500 units of a commodity at $40 each for customers and assumes the risk of selling them, or whether those 500 customers have directly and expressly commissioned him to buy the 500 units for their accounts at $40 each. In both cases, there is a demand to purchase 500 units at $40 each. And the material basis of the demand in each case is the wants of 500 individuals who are not physically present but are economically represented. The only difference is that, in one case, they are represented knowingly and on their own account, while, in the other case, though the dealer acts as their representative, he does so without their knowledge and for his own account and at his own risk.

The dealers' appraisals of exchange value are derived from the use values ascribed by their absent customers. The absentees' placing of use value as well as that of the buyers who are physically present is based on direct marginal utility. Hence these cases do not in any way vitiate the result previously formulated. It remains true throughout all variations of our problem that everything depends ultimately on the *direct marginal utility which the economic good has for the buyers, or on their conditions of demand and supply in the respective goods category.*

At this point, we need not embark upon a price analysis of complementary goods, capital goods, etc., which presents considerable complications. The proper place for such an analysis is with the special price problems, especially with the great problems of income distribution.[8]

3. *The Subjective Value of the Medium of Exchange for the Buyers.*

Whenever the medium of exchange for one good is some other good, as in the case of barter, the valuation discussed in point 2 is equally valid. Media of exchange usually are in the form of *money*. And because money can be made to serve equally well in all categories of want, its marginal utility and value do not depend on the relationship between want and satisfaction in any single category of want, but rather on how well individuals are provided in all their wants. In general, the subjective value of a unit of money is smaller for the rich and greater for the poor. But it should be noted that the important point here is not the absolute amount of wealth or of income, but rather the relationship of wealth and income to the wants of the individuals concerned.[9] There are some special circumstances that can influence the subjective value of money. Frivolity and prodigality depress it, the urgent necessity of making important payments makes cold cash more precious. Even the richest merchant, confronted by the necessity for meeting pressing obligations when his till is depleted, will certainly practice retrenchment in the matter of luxuries, such as precious paintings.

4. *The Quantity of the Good that is for Sale.*

To complete the price determinants, we must go back to the quantity in which the good is or will be available in the whole market area. It is not uncommon to conclude purchases of commodities not yet in existence, such as grain to be gathered in

---

[8] Cf. above, Part I of this essay, sections V and VI.

[9] Cf. above, Part I, p. 44.

the next harvest, or goods to be delivered upon completion of manufacture at some future time. If we pursue the causal chain one link further backward, we perceive that the quantity of goods available in a given market is determined by a variety of factors. These factors may include purely natural conditions, as in the purchase and sale of land, or in transactions involving natural produce, where the abundance of supply depends on how harvests turn out. Or they may include conditions that are purely *social and legal*, such as monopolies, cartels, coalitions, and the like. Or they may include the *costs of production*, a factor that finds particularly wide applicability. The higher the cost of producing a good, the smaller, comparatively, is the number of units produced for the satisfaction of demand, and vice versa. This is true for a number of readily understandable reasons which we shall examine later. At any rate, the influence on the available quantity of a given good constitutes the starting point for determining why costs exert their generally recognized influence on the prices of goods.

The total number of available units of a good constitutes the primary basic material for a market. What portion is actually brought to market depends on the subjective valuation of the commodity and medium of exchange by their owners. The situation is analogous to the one pointed out in connection with the quantities of a commodity desired by potential buyers. That is to say, there is no fixed barrier between that part of the total supply which its possessors regard as being for sale and that part which they consider as "not for sale." Any change in the relation of these subjective valuations, or even in the market price, can convert a quantity of goods which, the moment before, its owners described as "not for sale" into goods that are thrown into the market.

5. *The Subjective Value of the Good for the Sellers.*

Our discussions in section 2 apply also to this section. We should emphasize, however, that in our system of division of labor and entrepreneurial production the sellers possess goods in quantities that exceed by far their personal use. Hence, direct marginal utility and subjective use value of the goods are *usually very low* for these persons. Under such conditions, even a nominal return may be more advantageous than to hold on to the goods. This explains why, under unfavorable market conditions, sellers occasionally must sell their inventories at emergency and cut-rate prices. But even these emergency and giveaway prices exceed the subjective use value which the good possesses for them.

6. *The Subjective Value of the Medium of Exchange for the Sellers.*

This point is similar to what has already been stated above with reference to point 3, the subjective value of the medium of exchange for the buyers. But it happens even more often to sellers than to buyers that their general wealth does not determine their valuation of money but rather their special demand for cash. There are times when manufacturers or merchants are obliged to meet very pressing money obligations or indeed are tottering on the brink of bankruptcy. At such moments, they place especially high value on the medium of exchange, money, and for that reason are compelled to reconcile themselves to accepting small amounts of money for the goods they offer for sale. Herein lies part of the explanation of inordinately low prices at forced sales or in economic crises.

Four of these six price-determining factors concern the economic good and two (the third and sixth) the *medium of exchange*. The former are characteristic of economic goods regardless of the medium of exchange used; the latter affect every medium of exchange differently. They are significant only for the concrete question of how many of a certain medium of exchange can be obtained for a good? This is the question of *price*. The former retain their significance for the exchange ratio of our good towards all conceivable exchange goods, in fact, *they are the determining factors of exchange power or the objective exchange value of goods.*

As our analysis demonstrated above, those four factors (number of demands for the good, quantity of available units, subjective valuations by buyers and sellers) have a common root: *the demand for and supply of the economic good*. Both subjective value and objective exchange power have their ultimate root in demand and supply. Subjective value has its root in the individual economy, objective exchange power in the whole market, that is, in the *social* conditions of demand and supply.

When we identify these social conditions as the ultimate cause of exchange value, we must expressly reject a thought that is usually connected with this concept. It is true, exchange value has its roots in those conditions, but *by no means is there a precise proportional correlation*. Any given good's exchange value need not vary precisely or approximately with the average demand and supply conditions of society. The ultimate factors, that is, wants and goods supplies, do not directly contribute to the formation of price. Making their appearance in combinations, they can act only in groups, which suppresses the influence of many individual factors. This is like the mechanism that is driven by a number of elastic springs. Its effective force need not be proportional to the total number and strength of all its springs, for some inner springs may merely work to regulate and compensate for the others.

Similar conditions exist in the determination of price. At first, wants and goods supplies combine in individual action and work as groups through a person's subjective valuation. It could be that the possession of one hundred units is valued no differently and, therefore, exerts no more influence in the market than the possession of only 10 units in another combination. The subjective valuations exert an uneven influence on the formation of price; some are rendered completely ineffective; others exhaust their effects in mutual neutralization. And only the smallest third group, the valuations of the marginal pairs, decides the outcome.

This explains why, on the one hand, unequal prices may occur with equal average supply conditions, and on the other hand, equal prices may occur with unequal social supply conditions.[10] Therefore, it is not possible to deduce the supply conditions of society and also the welfare significance of an economic good for

---

[10] Let us assume, for instance, that an equal number of people desire an economic good with equal average intensity, let us say, with an average valuation of $10, and that an equal number, let us say, 1,000 units, is for sale. The price may differ greatly depending on the different combinations of those factors in "society." For instance, if all 1,000 buyers attach nearly equal value to a good so that the upward or downward deviations do not exceed $1, the price must approximate the valuations of the last buyers, that is, $9. But with the same valuation average of $10, if the first buyers attach a very high value and the last a very low value, for instance, $2, the price can then be no higher than $2. On the other hand, there can be a change in the general balance of social supply conditions without a change in price. For instance, price may not change at all, if the number of potential buyers or sellers or the level of their subjective valuations tends to rise but, by chance, this rise takes place among the excluded buyers or sellers or excluded valuations that neutralize each other.

society from the height of exchange value. It is erroneous, as I mentioned above,[11] to interpret the objective exchange value as the value for the *national economy*.

This does not mean that we will not *frequently* observe an approximate proportionality between the height of prices and social supply conditions. This is obvious. Even according to the principles of probability, it is likely that a small number of intense valuations will influence a particular area. When it is raining in the whole area, a single house cannot remain dry. And if the whole world urgently needs a certain good, it is very likely that individuals whose valuations influence the position of the marginal pair will need it more urgently and attach greater value than before. But there is no inevitability. This is why the price theory must not rest with defining demand and supply conditions and utility and scarcity in general as the ultimate determinants of the height of exchange value. It cannot and must not neglect developing the basic elements from which emerges the subjective valuation according to the law of marginal utility, and from them the price and exchange values according to the analogous law of marginal pairs.

---

[11] Above, p. 52.

V

FACTS AND FALLACIES IN THE LAW OF "SUPPLY AND DEMAND"

It is said that goods prices are governed by "the relationship of supply and demand."

This statement is true as long as we think not only of the *number* of desired and offered units but also of the totality of causes on the part of the prospective sellers and buyers. But since the statement reveals very little on both the nature of these causes and the manner of their effectiveness, it is by itself merely a title, a catchword, but not an economic law. We must search for the law in the precise explanations given by theorists who use the formula.

In fact, the older price theory already felt the need for a more precise determination of its formula. Two different explanations were offered. One meant to shed light on various real factors or "determinants" that exert their influence on price under the general label of "supply and demand." The other meant to define the relationship between all those factors and the level of price. In other words, the first explanation names the individual factors of price determination, the second develops the principle of their cooperation.

The attempts at the latter met with various results.[1] A remark

---

[1] At times these attempts have failed completely, which is all the more remarkable in a textbook by Roscher. Considering the great number of writers who present the theory of supply and demand, I gladly forego complete enumeration of quotations. Therefore, in the following, I shall consider only those three works that completely dominated the price theory in Germany up to the appearance of Schönberg's *Handbuch* and, therefore, can be considered as typical for the older theory: Hermann's *Staatswirtschaftliche Untersuchungen* (1st ed.,
(continued...)

made by Professor Rau was most unfortunate. According to him, "If supply and demand are approximately equal, the economic good is sold at a *medium price* that is advantageous to both parties."[2] This statement is erroneous if it covers the excluded would-be buyers and sellers who remain without influence. In this case, price attains a medium level even though ten times more goods may be desired than offered. But if we do not include these would-be candidates, supply and demand must always be equal, no matter whether price happens to be medium, or high, or low.

Another formulation is much better. It states that price "at any rate is that amount at which demand and supply are equal after some would-be candidates have withdrawn."[3] This formula is both correct and precise. In fact, the buyer's bidding must come to a halt and price is set when an equal number of buyers and sellers remains after exclusion of the least capable candidates. Nevertheless, the formula is not perfect; it is open to ambiguity. It speaks of an equality of supply and demand when equal quantities are desired and offered, no matter how unequal the intensity of demand and supply may be. Such concepts are merely quantitative and therefore unusable. Prices depend not only on the number of offered and desired units but also on the intensities of demand and supply. The general formula (that the relationship between supply and demand rules price) thus can be upheld only if the words "supply and demand" are interpreted in such a way that the special formulation is wrong. And the latter is correct only if interpreted in such a way that the general formula is fallacious. Both formulations cannot exist side by side unless we practice prestidigitation with the terms

---

[1] (...continued)
1832), Rau's *Grundsätze der Volkswirtschaftslehre* (8th ed., 1868) and Roscher's *Grundlagen der Nationalökonomie*. I am quoting from an older edition of this work that was written when Roscher's work completely and nearly alone dominated the German textbook market. (10th ed. 1873)

[2] Rau, *ibid.* Vol. I, Section 155.

[3] Also Rau, *ibid.*, strangely in the same section that contains the unfortunate formulation mentioned above. It is yet better and sharper with Mill, *Principles of Political Economy*, in German by Soetbeer, Leipzig, 1869, Book III, Chapter II, Section 4.

supply and demand.[4]

Let us now turn towards the other explanation that deals with individual "determinants."

The strength of *demand* is said to depend on two factors: its scope and its intensity. The scope of demand is expressed by the quantity of desired units.[5] Since it was recognized, however, that some part of demand remains without influence on the determination of price, a distinction was made between *effective* and *ineffective* demand. Not all the demand, but only the effective demand is said to influence price. And effective demand was defined as that demand which is supported by *the candidates' ability to pay.*[6]

This is quite correct except for one point: this is the borderline between effective and ineffective demand. The area of the latter is much too small in one direction and somewhat too large in another direction. We may remember that all excluded candidates are without influence on prices. But there are two reasons for being excluded: either the medium of exchange is valued too highly because we do not have enough -- for this category of "ineffective" demand we may use the attribute "inability to pay" which is a designation not entirely applicable but nevertheless accept-able -- or we may attach no specially high value to the acquisition of the economic good. The most capable millionaire will permit less affluent lovers of paintings to outbid him at an auction and his demand to be rendered "ineffective" if his subjective valuation of the painting is so much lower than that of the "enthusiastic" competitor. In the definition mentioned above the second category is not considered at all, which renders the area of ineffective demand much too narrow.

The area goes a little too far in the other direction. We must remember one of the excluded candidates, in fact, the most capable among them. He definitely influences prices which must be high

---

[4] Professor Neumann (*ibid.*, p. 288 *et seq.*) severely criticizes the "logical error" usually made in the popular formulation. But he uses some arguments with which I cannot fully agree.

[5] Hermann, *ibid.*, p. 67; Rau, *ibid.*, p. 204; Roscher, *ibid.*, Sec. 101.

[6] Hermann, p. 72, Rau, p. 204, Roscher, Sec. 104.

enough to exclude his subjective valuation. His demand is effective for the determination of price. To be sure, it is an insignificant exception to the rule that only the demand which is able to pay is effective.

Let us continue. The second factor that is said to determine demand is *intensity*. No objection can be raised here as long as we interpret the word intensity in the following manner. Intensity must not be understood as the *impulse of the desire to buy* but as the *willingness to buy at a higher price, if this were necessary*. It is obvious that the two are not identical. A laborer's wife who urgently needs a Sunday roast for her undernourished children will want to purchase it much more fervently than the prosperous burgher's wife who goes to the market at the same time. The former's urgency of desire to purchase unfortunately does not turn into willingness to pay a higher price because of the scarcity of cash, which makes the demand by the burgher's wife more "intensive." Surely, representatives of the prevailing doctrine usually understood this factor of "intensity," although they defined it incorrectly at times.[7]

The intensity of demand in turn is determined by the cooperation of two factors. The prevailing doctrine names *1. the value of the economic good for the individual desiring it,*[8] and *2. his ability to pay.*[9] The latter is explained as the possession of means for the purchase of the good,[10] which in turn is based on the would-be buyers' situation of wealth and income.[11]

---

[7] For instance, Prof. Rau, who defines the intensity as "strength of the desire to purchase." But then he adds "from which merges the inclination to grant the other party favorable conditions," which indicates that he is moving at least approximately in the right direction.

[8] Hermann, p. 67, Rau, p. 196, Roscher, Section 102.

[9] Hermann, p. 72, Rau, p. 204, Roscher, Section 104.

[10] Hermann, p. 72.

[11] According to Hermann, p. 72, the ability to pay off the would-be buyer depends "at times on income, and at other times on their capitals"; Professor Rau p. 204 named directly the "wealth situation" rather than the ability to pay; in order to illustrate the different degrees of ability to pay, Professor Roscher confronts "proletariat," "well-to-do" and "rich people." Sec. 104. Cf. also Schäffle, *Ges. System*, 3rd ed., Vol. 1, p. 173.

Except for a small imperfection in detail,[12] the first factor is quite correct, the latter basically fallacious. Instead of "ability to pay," it should be "the value of the medium of exchange for the would-be buyer." It is true, in many cases both expressions practically coincide. But in some cases they do not, which makes the formula "ability to pay" positively fallacious. In order to prove my point, I would like to present several such cases.

Above all, the ability-to-pay theory is inapplicable to all cases of *barter* which, too, must be properly explained by the general price theory. For instance, an antique dealer proposes to exchange a beautiful bust, which I would like to acquire, for old coins in my possession. It is obvious that I shall offer all the more coins for the bust the lower I value the coins, and vice versa. We thus encounter a determinant for the intensity of demand that obviously has nothing whatever to do with my "ability to pay" but is identical with the determinant "value of the medium of exchange for the buyer."

The same may happen also with money prices. For instance, in a country with paper money a buyer fears or anticipates that the paper money will soon be devalued. His desire to quickly dispose of the endangered notes may lead him to a higher money bid for a piece of land or a house. The reason for his higher bidding obviously does not lie in the value of the house or lot, nor in his ability to pay, but simply in the lower value which he attaches to the medium of exchange, the paper money.

Furthermore, it is a well-known fact that frivolous individuals and spendthrifts frequently squander their money on the most superfluous things. In our technical language, they exert an "intensive" demand for many things they happen to come across. What causes this "intensity"? Certainly not the high subjective value which they ascribe to the economic good! For they pay large sums even for things they do not need, which cannot possibly have high use value for them. And it cannot be their

---

[12] I contend, for instance, that Roscher (Sec. 102) too narrowly defines use value, while Hermann, (p. 67) and Rau (p. 204 in connection with p. 196) do consider the exchange value but contribute nearly nothing to the solution of the difficulty in explaining price and exchange value of an economic good from the "exchange value" itself.

exceptional "ability to pay," for they often display frantic desires even after their wealth is already spent and they are running into debt. It is obvious that the true reason is the low valuation which these people attach to the medium of exchange.

Although I am emphasizing several points in which the ability-to-pay theory proves fallacious, I readily admit that it appears to apply to most cases. In fact, in order to refute it in practical examples, I had to cite several exceptional cases. It is very informative now to disclose the reason. The ability to pay, or better yet, individual affluence, is not the only determinant for the *valuation of money* although it is the preponderant one. As we know,[13] other conditions being equal, money has lower value for rich people than for poor people. It is quite natural that people with the highest ability to pay are also willing to sacrifice the greatest amount of money.

Consequently, it may thus be stated that prevailing theory names a reason of the reason instead of the reason itself. It is indeed an important reason that applies to many cases. But it is only one of several possible reasons. The truth is that the intensity of demand depends not only on the value of the economic good but also on the value of the medium of exchange for the buyer. And if this last factor is to be explained, we may name the buyer's situation of wealth as an important secondary reason.

Let us now turn from demand to supply.

According to prevailing doctrine, supply, too, is determined by its *size* and *intensity*. Size is defined as the quantity of economic goods offered for sale. According to a limiting clause, the supply must be *effective*. But this characteristic is explained even less fortunately than "effective demand." According to Professor Rau,[14] "effective supply is the supply meant and offered for sale." We object on the grounds that the offers of all excluded would-be sellers remain ineffective for the determination of price, except for that of the marginal pair, no matter how sincere their offers may be. Except for this unfortunate explanation, we can raise no further objections against the determinant "size of effective supply." And

---

[13] Cf. above p. 44.

[14] P. 204.

we cannot object to the second determinant "intensity of supply," assuming it does not mean the urgency of the desire to sell but rather the inclination, even without urgency, to sell possibly at lower prices. We object strenuously to the manner in which prevailing doctrine develops the deeper reasons for the intensity itself. As we stated above,[15] the intensity, or more precisely, the figure down to which the seller may continue his offers, depends on the cooperation of two circumstances: the value of the medium of exchange for the seller and his valuation of the economic good that must be relinquished. The seller will settle on fewer media of exchange the greater the value he attaches to these media and the lower the value of the economic good in his possession. Prevailing doctrine again develops correctly the first of these determinants;[16] it presents the second less cogently, and finally, adds a third one that is completely misplaced, namely, the *costs* of the good.

Professor Hermann develops the second determinant relatively well. He mentions, although merely occasionally, that, in the case of "simple and isolated exchange," the seller considers the use value while, in "society," he reflects on the exchange value of the good offered (p. 76 *et seq*.) He then interrupts this thought to demonstrate the influence of cost on price. But later he returns to it (p. 88), to be sure, under a different title ("other sales prices"). He then elaborates in detail that the seller will never relinquish his good at a lower price than he may obtain in another market from another buyer, which means that he will never relinquish the good for less than the *exchange value* which he himself ascribes to it. We only reprove that Professor Hermann is bogged down in the formula (p. 89), that "the price of a good is determined, other conditions being equal, by other sales prices." He thereby explains one market price with another instead of tracing it back to its fundamental determinants.

Professor Roscher's explanation is even less satisfactory. In obvious reference to Hermann, he once mentions the seller's consideration of the use or exchange value of his good (section

---

[15] Sec. IV, p. 509 *et seq*.

[16] Hermann, p. 92 *et seq*. Rau p. 204, "the stronger or weaker desire of sellers to dispose of their goods can be conceived as the present concrete valuation of the money received." Less clearly by Roscher, Sec. 105.

105). But where he enumerates the "ultimate conditions" on which supply and demand themselves depend (section 101), he forgets to mention the value of the economic good for the seller, and thus reveals the low importance he attaches to this factor for the explanation of price. Professor Rau completely overlooks the seller's value for the good, inasmuch as he deduces the intensity of supply merely from man's valuation of the medium of exchange.[17]

In popular doctrine the scanty consideration given to the value of the economic good for the seller has been replaced in a quite dubious manner by a third factor, consideration of *costs*.[18] It cannot be denied that there is an important connection between costs and price, which the theory of price must investigate in detail. But *this is not the place for it*, which deals with the *intensity* of supply. It is positively fallacious to appeal to costs as determinant or as "minimal limit" for the asking price of sellers. Costs constitute no necessary economic limit, which the countless sales under costs reveal every day in every city, such as, bankruptcy sales, liquidation sales of articles that went out of fashion, etc. The seller never takes less than what the economic good is worth to him, but he frequently takes less than it has cost him. However, I readily admit that in a certain sense the seller will be mindful of his costs: he hates to see prices decline below them. Cost is no determinant on his scale of price; it is a demarcation point at which the desired profit turns to loss. Costs merely reflect, so to speak, a kind of sentimentality to which we must not yield in the market place. To pass one's level of costs has no more significance than, for instance, the lowering of price below a point at which offers were made to us in the past but then rejected by us. If we remember this price, we may hesitate to drop lower, but it may be smart to do so if market conditions demand it.

The case is as follows : If, at this time, we cannot cover our costs in this market, we may hope to cover them in another market in the future. Of course, harboring this hope, we will not sell at this time. The determining factor is not that we will not take less than cost, but that we will not take less than we can obtain *in another*

[17] *Ibid*., p. 204.

[18] Hermann p. 76 - 88; Roscher, Sec. 101, 106 *et seq*.

market. In other words, we will not take less than the exchange value which we ascribe to our good, rightly or wrongly. Conversely, we may have no such hope to obtain more in another market. Then we immediately reduce our offer below the level of costs down to the true margin that reflects our own valuation of the good. If we cannot obtain more than $800 for a good that has cost us $1000 and is worth no more than $100, we would obviously be foolish to stubbornly adhere to our costs and not sell the good for $800. Such stubbornness would cost us $700, which is the difference between the rejected bid and the use value of the unsold good to us.[19]

The most important influence of costs on the determination of price is exerted at a different place: it is not the level of price, nor the intensity of supply, but quite simply the number of produced units and thus the volume of supply. If the cost of an economic good declines from $10 to $5, it is very likely that also its price will also decline to $5. The reason is not that the sellers are ready to reduce their goods to $5 a unit, which in emergencies they would have done even at a cost of $10 per unit. The reason is that the reduction of costs makes it economically possible to produce more units that will be offered with equal or nearly equal intensity as before. Therefore, the proper place for the consideration of costs in supply and demand is with regard to the enumeration of *secondary determinants for the quantity of supply*. This is where we, too, mentioned costs. But since costs have given rise to so many particular relations, it appears advisable to reserve an independent

---

[19] Costs affect directly the intensity of supply in a single case: namely, when we are concerned with the supply of goods that will be delivered in the future and that must be produced in the meantime. For the acceptance of such an order the production costs definitely constitute a lower limit. But upon closer examination, also this case can be reduced to the effectiveness of goods value as determinant. For it is not the finished product that is sold from inventory and on which the calculations are based, but it is the totality of producers' goods which the manufacturer is contracting to employ on behalf of the buyer. Of course, the manufacturer will not promise to do so, if the buyer's medium of exchange is not more valuable than the producers' goods that must be sacrificed. This is why the "height of costs," which are identical with the value of "producers' goods," constitutes the lower limit of price. This is not so because costs principally constitute a determinant of price, but because the producers' goods now constitute the true object of sale due to the concrete circumstances of the case.

presentation for them. This is why we merely mention costs in a cursory fashion above, and analyze them *ex professo* in the final section below.

Let us draw conclusions from our critical analysis.

The general formula that supply and demand rules price is *true but vague*. It is *true* and *precise* to say, although afflicted with technological ambiguity, that price is set at the very point at which supply and demand are equal. It is *true* that supply and demand are determined by their quantity and intensity. The popular limitation of effective demand is *imprecise*, that of effective supply is *incorrect*. But it is *correct* to name, as the first ultimate determinant of the supply intensity, the value of the medium of exchange. The popular explanation of the second determinant, the value of the economic good for the seller, is rather *unsatisfactory*. And *positively incorrect at this place* is the appeal to costs as the third determinant.

Let us also add that the manner in which these doctrines are presented also lacks in clarity and sagacity. Almost no single concept used by the doctrine is defined precisely and without ambiguity, neither supply and demand, nor their effectiveness, intensity, or ability to pay. In spite of the large volume of discussion of the individual determinants, there is an exceptionally poor treatment of the manner in which these determinants cooperate as a whole and thus determine price. The total picture is rather unpleasant: *the truth is mixed with half-truths and errors and combined into a loose whole with little inner clarity*.

It cannot surprise us, therefore, that a profound and sagacious man like Neumann completely doubts that a healthy fruit can be reaped from such a sick doctrine. To escape the countless errors and misunderstandings, he sincerely advises us to renounce completely the whole price law of supply and demand.[20]

Shall we agree to such a surrender? Certainly not. For thousands of years the price of grain has fallen after good harvests and risen after bad ones. As certain as this is the case, so certain is the law of supply and demand, the explanation of which economic theory cannot escape. We need not abandon the doctrine of supply

---

[20] Schönberg's *Handbuch*, 2nd ed., Vol. I, p. 286 et seq.

and demand, merely reform it. We must give new content to an old formula. I believe that this is not so difficult after all. Inasmuch as the shortcomings of the old theory resulted from a single point, they can be overcome also at this point: *we must place into the very center of our doctrine the thought that price is nothing but the product of subjective valuations of people.* This solves all our problems. Many old determinants are confirmed, others are corrected. The useful but ambiguous concepts of "intensity", "effectiveness," etc., receive a sharp and clear delineation, and the cooperation and coordination of the various co-determinants receive inner connection and logical order. Finally, the formula of the "valuations of the marginal pairs" provides a definite and irrefutable criterion for the price that results from all these individual factors.

It is characteristic, indeed, that the thought of explaining all price phenomena from subjective valuations already occurred to the representatives of the old price theory. Professor Rau once said "*It is obvious that concrete value is the main force in both supply and demand.*"[21] At that time, the theory of subjective value had not yet been developed fully in order to serve as a perfected tool for an explanation of prices. There were some successes, but price could not yet be explained. In order to close the gaps, it was necessary to call on quite heterogeneous determinants. But it is rather characteristic again that every step in this direction was accompanied by misfortune. The writers did not move too far from the truth nor did they have much success. They became imprecise, unclear, incorrect, particularly in all matters pertaining to "ability to pay," to "costs" as determinant of intensity, the explanation of effective demand and supply, and, finally, the comprehensive formulation of the price law. In fact, it may be said that all that is good and meritorious in the doctrine of supply and demand mainly and substantially explains price from subjective value. And all that is incomplete and dubious is so because it fails to draw its explanation from this very source.

---

[21] *Grundsätze der Volkswirtschaftslehre*, 8th ed., Sec. 154, Note e.

VI
THE LAW OF COSTS

The market price of goods that can be reproduced at will tends to coincide in the long run with the production costs. The reason is as follows. In the long run, the market price of such goods can neither be much higher nor much lower than their costs. If, at any time, the price should rise greatly above costs, production of such goods would become especially profitable for businessmen. They would be induced to expand their flourishing production, and new businessmen would be encouraged to enter the profitable industry. This would increase the product supply in the market and cause prices to decline according to the law of supply and demand. If, on the other hand, the market price should fall below costs, continuation of production inflicts losses. Many businessmen now abandon production or curtail it, which in turn will reduce the product supply in the market and ultimately, according to the law of supply and demand, cause an increase in market prices. This, in brief, is the content of the *law of costs* as we encounter it in life and literature.

I cannot enter into a discussion of a number of questions that would lead us into many detailed analyses. I cannot discuss whether production costs or reproduction costs are decisive, and in case of differences of costs, whether the highest, lowest, or medium costs are relevant, and what is to be included in costs. Such discussions can be found in every textbook, treated in detail and mostly correctly. At this point, we are merely interested in *the law of costs relative to price theory*.

We should like to note that the law of costs is not a general price law in addition to that of supply and demand; it is instead a *particular* law within the latter.

It is a limited price law. For it is well known that it encompasses only those economic goods *that can be reproduced at will*. Many important categories of goods as, for instance, all land and monopoly goods, are permanently excluded. This is why I disagree with Professor Neumann who assigns the position of "the most general" price law to the law of costs.[1] Such a position can be understood only if we remember that Professor Neumann completely rejects the "so-called" law of supply and demand, which fact then elevates the law of costs in his world to the rank of *relatively* general law, in spite of its limited validity.

Furthermore, the law of costs does not stand outside the law of supply and demand, nor in opposition to it. It stands within it. It merely contains a particular regularity, which it assumes everywhere and from which it derives its force. In fact, there could be no law of costs without the law of supply and demand. It is impossible to defend the former without appealing to the functioning of the latter. I am calling on scholars who disagree to demonstrate another foundation.

In this situation, the position of Professor Neumann, who denies the law of supply and demand and thus also the law of costs, appears to be untenable because it is contradictory. It cannot be denied that price and cost are made to coincide because every deviation of price causes an adjustment in supply and demand which in turn moves price toward cost. Obviously, the regularity of the adjusting factor can be no less than that of the adjustments themselves. And if it is admitted that the effect, which is the coincidence of cost and price, is regular enough to earn the label of regularity, then this attribute cannot be denied to the very cause, which is the operation of supply and demand.

It is even stranger in this connection that Professor Neumann, and he is not alone,[2] wants to use certain cases in which the goods

---

[1] Schönberg's *Handbook*, 2nd ed., p. 286.

[2] I frequently argue here and in this essay against my esteemed colleague from Tübingen. I do so not because I differ more widely from his opinion than from others, but merely on account of the high esteem he enjoys in all questions of price theory. I deem it, therefore, important to cope especially and thoroughly (continued...)

obviously follow the law of costs as proof against the validity of the law of supply and demand. He believes that in certain cases price tends to change when costs alone change without similar changes in supply and demand. And this is said to prove that such a determination of price is not ruled by the relations of supply and demand. Whoever is familiar with both price laws will expect, right from the beginning, that an error has crept into such examples. In fact, it can be proven easily in all such cases that, in spite of all appearance to the contrary, changes took place not only in costs but also in the relationship of supply and demand.[3]

Having just rejected several objections, I myself would like to raise one that must be removed before our thesis can claim safety. If goods obey the law of costs, I contend, they do not cease to obey also the law of supply and demand. According to our version of the latter, price is determined by *the subjective valuations of the economic good by buyers and sellers.* But the law of costs contends that price is determined by *production costs*. Do not both sentences contradict each other?

There is no contradiction. Just as there was no contradiction in the subjective value theory between the proposition that marginal utility determines subjective value and the other proposition that costs determine subjective value! The train of thought that solved the apparent contradiction in that case is very similar here. The difficulty in solving the apparent contradiction lies in the fact that many interrelationships are involved in the interaction of exchange and the application of the concept from the individual to society. If we simplify and look through the interrelationships that tend to complicate the matter in practical life, we arrive at the following

---

[2] (...continued)
with his opinion.

[3] Professor Neumann, (*ibid.*, p. 289) presents an example "of an equal demand for uniforms that are needed in equal quantities but manufactured usually only upon order. If the production costs of these uniforms rise, price will usually rise although there is no change in supply and demand." Is it true that supply had not changed? Let us assume that 200 uniforms are needed and offered at the present cost of $100. But now costs rise to $110. The result is that no one can accept an order at $100. At a price of $100, 200 uniforms were formerly offered, and now not a single uniform at the same price. Is it true that supply has not changed?

interaction between value, price, and cost.

The determination of value and price takes its point of departure *from the subjective valuations of finished products by their consumers*. They determine the demand for these products, which at first faces the ready supply of finished products in the hands of producers. The intersection of the consumers' and producers' valuations, which reflects the valuation of the marginal pairs, determines the price. It does so separately for all categories of products. For instance, the price of steel rails is determined by the conditions of supply and demand for rails, the price for nails by the conditions of supply and demand for nails, and, in the same way, the price of all products that are manufactured by those of their producers' goods. In order to clarify the matter as much as possible, let us assume that the relations of supply and demand are quite different with various steel products and consequently also their initial prices. And let us assume that the price of a certain quantity of goods that can be manufactured from one and the same unit of producers' goods, as for instance one hundredweight of steel,[4] fluctuates between $1 in the cheapest goods category and $10 in the most expensive one.

Now the market price which every producer may obtain determines his subjective *exchange value* which he may place on his product.[5] And because the value of a product is decisive for the value of his *means of production*,[6] every producer appraises a production unit, in our example the hundredweight of steel, as highly as the market price of the products that are made from the unit. The manufacturer of the cheapest product thus will appraise it at $1, another at $2, the third at $3, etc. and, finally, the manufacturer of the most expensive product at $10.[7]

---

[4] For reasons of simplicity I shall not enter into a discussion of the cooperation of complementary producers' goods at this point.

[5] See Part I, p. 59.

[6] Cf. above, p. 72.

[7] If I had not disregarded the cooperation of other means of production, for instance, labor, tools, fuels, etc. I would have to ascribe a part of product value to the cooperating goods according to the principles of the value of complementary goods developed above (Part I, p. 63.). I would have to assign only a share of

(continued...)

Guided by these appraisals, every producer enters the market to buy the necessary steel for his continuing production. His *volume* of demand is determined by the quantity of goods he hopes to sell. And his intensity is determined by the valuation described above: everyone will be willing to bid as much for a unit of producers' goods as he can obtain from his sales to his own customers. That is to say, one will be willing to bid as much as $1, the other $2, and finally the last one $10 for one hundredweight of steel. This demand is met by a supply of steel inventories in warehouses and steel mills. The supplies now are transferred into the possession of the most capable buyers at a price that falls between the valuations of the last effective buyer and the first excluded buyer. If the valuations of many would-be buyers are close, which happens regularly in large markets, the leeway then is so narrow that price is set very close to the valuation of the last buyer. We may therefore consider this valuation as a guidepost for prices. Let us assume that the buyer who attaches a value of $3 to one hundredweight of steel is the last buyer and thus the market price is set at $3. The following consideration is then appropriate.

The price of the production good, steel, is first determined by the *last buyer's valuation*, which in turn is determined by the *market price of his product*. A special circumstance characterizes this product. If the price of one hundredweight of steel is $3, only those products with a market price of at least $3 can be produced. Manufacture of all products of lesser value becomes economically unfeasible. The product with a market price of $3, that is, the last and least valuable product for which the steel can still be used economically, is the marginal product. The same regularity that rules subjective value thus also rules prices. *Just as the subjective value of producers' goods depends on the value of the least valuable or marginal product, so does the price of the marginal product rule the price of the means of production.*

We may draw several conclusions from this. Manufacturing of products whose prices exceed $3 receive a premium that causes

---

[7] (...continued)
product value to the steel. The same relations as between the value of steel and that of all its products would then prevail between the value of steel and that share of product value.

them to expand their production and enlarge the supply. The more the supply is expanded the lower falls the equilibrium point between supply and demand. And thus the valuations of the decisive marginal pairs drop until finally the price reaches $3. This eliminates the premium for manufacturers and the incentive to further expand production. On the other hand, those products whose market price is lower than $3 cannot be manufactured at all. If there is no demand at $3, the products will never be produced. But if at least one buyer is willing to bid $3, a temporary curtailment in production and thereby a reduction in supply will raise the price to $3, and regular production can be pursued. Thus, through the mediation of subjective valuations that give rise to prices, all market prices of related products which at first stood higher than the price of the marginal product are reduced to the level of the marginal product, and all prices which at first stood lower are raised to that same level. The general relative relationship of cost and price is thereby restored.

Our analysis permits us to present the following principles on the relationship of cost and price:

1. *There is a general relative relationship of cost and price for all goods that can be reproduced at will.*

2. *By and large this relative relationship comes into existence in such a way that the product price is the ruling factor, and the price of producers' goods the one that is ruled.*[8]

3. *In particular, the price of the marginal product is decisive, that is, the least valuable product for which the producers' good can be economically employed.*

4. *Through the mediation of costs the prices of all other*

---

[8] If there should be any further doubt about this basic proposition of our theory, I would like to turn to a well-known experience. For instance, in a sudden boom of railroad construction the price of rails rises first and through them the price of the good, steel. Our theory naturally explains this phenomenon. The price boost of rails on account of the demand opens new profitable employment for steel. Those opportunities absorb a part of the steel supply which otherwise would have been used in other production. The least profitable production, of course, must stand back. The "marginal product" thus is lifted to a higher level, which raises the price of steel and then spreads to other steel products. The cause of this upwards movement clearly originated from the rising prices of the products.

production related goods adjust to this price.

5. *All this is brought about by the play of subjective valuations, respectively their resultants, so that the law of costs stands neither in opposition to nor separate from the laws of marginal utility and marginal pairs, but is encompassed by them.*

I conclude. A great deal more could be said, and no one knows better than I the gaps that remain in my presentation. This is why I am not pretending to offer a complete theory of value and price, of subjective and objective value. I merely hope to have pointed the way which in my belief leads to a complete and coherent theory. In spite of all the shortcomings of my attempt, I hope to have proven convincingly two things: (1) as far as purely economic motives are concerned, I hope to have proven that *a dualistic explanation of value and price phenomena from two different principles of "utility" and "costs" is neither necessary nor satisfactory* and that an explanation from a single principle is superior not only for reasons of outer simplicity but also from inner logic and irrefutable concurrence with the facts. And secondly, I hope to have proven that *this one principle from which we endeavor to explain everything is least artificial and most natural for any point of departure, and that it springs from the very nature of things. For it cannot be denied that cause and aim of all human economy lie in the greatest possible improvement of our well-being. And we deduce our behavior towards economic goods from this very significance they have for our well-being.*

INDEX

INDEX